INTRODUCIN
ISSUES WITH
OPPOSING
VIEWPOINTS®

W9-ATO-659

Witch Hunt or Justice? Accusations Against Public Figures

M. M. Eboch, Book Editor

GREENHAVEN
PUBLISHING

Published in 2019 by Greenhaven Publishing, LLC
353 3rd Avenue, Suite 255, New York, NY 10010

First Edition

Articles in Greenhaven Publishing anthologies are often edited for length to meet page requirements. In addition, original titles of these works are changed to clearly present the main thesis and to explicitly indicate the author's opinion. Every effort is made to ensure that Greenhaven Publishing accurately reflects the original intent of the authors. Every effort has been made to trace the owners of the copyrighted material.

Library of Congress Cataloging-in-Publication Data

Names: Eboch, M. M., editor.
Title: Witch hunt or justice? : accusations against public figures / MM
  Eboch, book editor.
Description: First edition. | New York : Greenhaven Publishing, 2019. |
  Series: Introducing issues with opposing viewpoints | Includes
  bibliographical references and index. | Audience: Grades 7–12.
Identifiers: LCCN 2018025436| ISBN 9781534504264 (library bound) | ISBN
  9781534504899 (pbk.)
Subjects: LCSH: Public opinion—Juvenile literature. | Reputation—Juvenile
  literature. | Celebrities—Public opinion—Juvenile literature. | Public
  officers—Public opinion—Juvenile literature.
Classification: LCC HM1236 .W58 2019 | DDC 303.3/8—dc23
LC record available at https://lccn.loc.gov/2018025436

Manufactured in the United States of America

Website: http://greenhavenpublishing.com

Contents

Foreword

Indulging in a wide spectrum of ideas, beliefs, and perspectives is a critical cornerstone of democracy. After all, it is often debates over differences of opinion, such as whether to legalize abortion, how to treat prisoners, or when to enact the death penalty, that shape our society and drive it forward. Such diversity of thought is frequently regarded as the hallmark of a healthy and civilized culture. As the Reverend Clifford Schutjer of the First Congregational Church in Mansfield, Ohio, declared in a 2001 sermon, "Surrounding oneself with only like-minded people, restricting what we listen to or read only to what we find agreeable is irresponsible. Refusing to entertain doubts once we make up our minds is a subtle but deadly form of arrogance." With this advice in mind, Introducing Issues with Opposing Viewpoints books aim to open readers' minds to the critically divergent views that comprise our world's most important debates.

Introducing Issues with Opposing Viewpoints simplifies for students the enormous and often overwhelming mass of material now available via print and electronic media. Collected in every volume is an array of opinions that captures the essence of a particular controversy or topic. Introducing Issues with Opposing Viewpoints books embody the spirit of nineteenth-century journalist Charles A. Dana's axiom: "Fight for your opinions, but do not believe that they contain the whole truth, or the only truth." Absorbing such contrasting opinions teaches students to analyze the strength of an argument and compare it to its opposition. From this process readers can inform and strengthen their own opinions, or be exposed to new information that will change their minds. Introducing Issues with Opposing Viewpoints is a mosaic of different voices. The authors are statespeople, pundits, academics, journalists, corporations, and ordinary people who have felt compelled to share their experiences and ideas in a public forum. Their words have been collected from newspapers, journals, books, speeches, interviews, and the Internet, the fastest growing body of opinionated material in the world.

Introducing Issues with Opposing Viewpoints shares many of the well-known features of its critically acclaimed parent series, Opposing

Viewpoints. The articles allow readers to absorb and compare divergent perspectives. Active reading questions preface each viewpoint, requiring the student to approach the material thoughtfully and carefully. Photographs, charts, and graphs supplement each article. A thorough introduction provides readers with crucial background on an issue. An annotated bibliography points the reader toward articles, books, and websites that contain additional information on the topic. An appendix of organizations to contact contains a wide variety of charities, nonprofit organizations, political groups, and private enterprises that each hold a position on the issue at hand. Finally, a comprehensive index allows readers to locate content quickly and efficiently.

Introducing Issues with Opposing Viewpoints is also significantly different from Opposing Viewpoints. As the series title implies, its presentation will help introduce students to the concept of opposing viewpoints and learn to use this material to aid in critical writing and debate. The series' four-color, accessible format makes the books attractive and inviting to readers of all levels. In addition, each viewpoint has been carefully edited to maximize a reader's understanding of the content. Short but thorough viewpoints capture the essence of an argument. A substantial, thought-provoking essay question placed at the end of each viewpoint asks the student to further investigate the issues raised in the viewpoint, compare and contrast two authors' arguments, or consider how one might go about forming an opinion on the topic at hand. Each viewpoint contains sidebars that include at-a-glance information and handy statistics. A Facts About section located in the back of the book further supplies students with relevant facts and figures.

Following in the tradition of the Opposing Viewpoints series, Greenhaven Publishing continues to provide readers with invaluable exposure to the controversial issues that shape our world. As John Stuart Mill once wrote: "The only way in which a human being can make some approach to knowing the whole of a subject is by hearing what can be said about it by persons of every variety of opinion and studying all modes in which it can be looked at by every character of mind. No wise man ever acquired his wisdom in any mode but this." It is to this principle that Introducing Issues with Opposing Viewpoints books are dedicated.

Introduction

"When one woman breaks the silence, others are empowered to tell their [stories]."

—Sonia Ossorio, president of the National Organization for Women–New York

\#MeToo—the hashtag that started a revolution. Although the movement gained fame in 2017, its history goes back to 2006. Tarana Burke, an African American civil rights activist, founded a nonprofit organization, Just Be Inc. She wanted to help victims of sexual harassment and assault, especially women and girls of color. She called her movement Me Too as a way to encourage empathy between women who had survived sexual harassment or assault. The movement did not immediately get widespread attention.

In 2017, #MeToo roared onto the social media stage. Several actresses accused Hollywood producer Harvey Weinstein of sexual harassment. Actress and activist Alyssa Milano responded with a tweet. It said, "If you've been sexually harassed or assaulted write 'me too' as a reply to this tweet." Stories of harassment and assault flooded social media, linked by the #MeToo hashtag. By this time, Twitter had over 300 million monthly active users. The hashtag spread to other platforms, with more than 12 million posts and reactions on Facebook in the first 24 hours. Two little words had set off a revolution.

How successful was #MeToo in changing the world? Some powerful men lost their jobs after they were publicly accused of sexual harassment or assault. These men were not being accused of anything new. Their behavior had gone on for years, but complaints had been ignored, covered up, or quickly forgotten.

That tolerance seemed to be at an end.

The movement spread from the entertainment business to other fields, from music to sports to politics. In the business world, men at the highest levels of power tumbled. Business leaders resigned at several companies, including Nike and Bank of America. Even charities were affected. Executives at the Humane Society, Save the Children, and Oxfam lost jobs. News companies posted lists of famous men and leaders accused of sexual harassment. The number soon passed 70, then 100.

The movement affected average men as well. Many worried about whether their behavior could be considered sexual harassment. Some took hard looks at their past behaviors and current habits. They listened to women. When necessary, they made changes to what they said and did. They promised to be better allies for the victims. (Sexual harassment and assault are most common by men against women. Still, both men and women can be victims of sexual harassment. Some of the recent accusations came from men against other men. Women can commit sexual harassment and assault, but thus far accusations have focused on men.)

Other men insisted that the movement had gone too far. They claimed that men wouldn't know how to behave in this new era. Could they ask a woman on a date? Could they shake her hand? They called #MeToo an attack that made all men into villains. They questioned the truth of some of the accusations. They even found a few proven cases of false rape claims to back their skepticism. What had happened to innocent until proven guilty? Even if some of these men were guilty, did they deserve the repercussions? What about their careers, their potential? Surely they deserved to be forgiven and given another chance.

In contrast, many people feel not enough has changed. A few powerful men lost their jobs when famous women accused them of harassment. But most of the women who suffer harassment are not famous. Their stories don't get as much attention. Women of color complained that they didn't get the same support as white women when they reported abuse. Change won't be enough until it protects the trans woman of color working as a janitor as well as the white celebrity.

Sexual harassment is still rampant in most fields. Some companies have made changes to their policies to better support potential victims. Other companies are content to deny or ignore the problem and hope it won't affect them. In a 2018 survey, 57 percent of business board members reported that they still hadn't discussed sexual misconduct or sexism in the workplace.

Even the powerful men who lost their jobs may not suffer for long. Within months, stories reported that many were planning their comebacks. Do these men deserve a second chance? Should they be forgiven if they apologize, or if they donate to a women's organization, or once they're suffered a certain amount? Or do they deserve to have their careers ended? Do the number of accusations matter, or the details of them? Can a man be forgiven for making inappropriate comments, but not for exposing himself or grabbing a woman's breast? Should every accused man suffer the same amount?

What if the accusations cannot be proven? Few sexual assault charges ever make it all the way through the court system. It's nearly impossible to get solid evidence about whether an interaction was consensual or not. The challenges are even greater when it comes to sexual harassment. Behavior may be inappropriate even when it is not illegal. It may be impossible to try someone in a court of law. Is the court of public opinion a good substitute?

It's worth noting that none of these men lost their positions because of one anonymous rumor. In most cases they were accused by multiple victims, sometimes dozens. Their behavior had lasted for years and was often well-known in their industries. In addition, their actions caused real harm. Many women have quit jobs because that was the only way they could find to end the sexual harassment they faced. Some left their career fields entirely. Actions have consequences, and an apology may not be enough to counteract those consequences.

Are some performers or artists so talented that we should appreciate their skills even if we deplore their personal behavior? Can we show the work of dead artists who were criminals but not living artists who have been accused of harassment? Is it more important for a CEO to run a company profitably, or to be a good person? Is it even possible to separate public success and private morality? Do we need these men anymore? What if women were not routinely ignored or refused the paths to success? Perhaps we'd have more than enough talent to take the place of the abusive men.

#MeToo is changing the world. Some people claim that's for the better, while others point out pitfalls. People argue about whether it has gone too far or not far enough. The contributors who offer their viewpoints in *Introducing Issues with Opposing Viewpoints: Witch Hunt or Justice? Accusations Against Public Figures*, shed light on this ongoing contemporary issue.

Chapter 1

Do Public Accusations Seek Justice or Destroy Lives?

In the wake of #MeToo, some men feel threatened that behavior that was considered acceptable in the past is now being called out.

One Voice Can Start a Revolution

"These women are not riding a wave for 15 minutes of fame; they are emboldened and empowered by the examples of other victims."

Nina Bahadur

In the following viewpoint, Nina Bahadur argues that one accusation of sexual assault often leads other victims to speak up. This viewpoint was written in the fall of 2017, shortly after *The New York Times* claimed that women had been accusing film producer Harvey Weinstein of sexual harassment for decades. Once the story broke, even more women publicly shared their stories of sexual harassment and assault by Weinstein. This encouraged women in other fields to speak up about their experiences. Within months, many powerful men had resigned or been fired due to accusations of sexual harassment or assault. Nina Bahadur is a freelance writer and editor.

AS YOU READ, CONSIDER THE FOLLOWING QUESTIONS:

1. Why do victims of sexual assault and harassment often keep quiet, according to the author?
2. Why do some skeptics accuse women of lying when they claim they are victims of harassment?
3. How can one person's accusations encourage others to speak up, according to the author?

"Do You Believe Me Now? Why Sexual Assault Allegations Come in Waves," by Nina Bahadur, *Condé Nast*, October 13, 2017. Reprinted by permission.

Actresses Ashley Judd and Mira Sorvino claim that Harvey Weinstein derailed their careers because they would not comply with his demands.

Over the last week, the story behind Harvey Weinstein's long reported history of sexual assault and harassment has unfurled like a soiled red carpet. After the *New York Times* published an explosive report on the subject, woman after woman has made public, disturbing allegations of sexual harassment and assault by the famous, powerful, and notoriously nasty producer. Each new sickening tale opens the door for more women to share their own. In such cases, people may wonder, Why now? Why, when these stories date back years, did the women not say anything until someone else did? The answer is inherent in the question itself—often it takes one loud voice to make it possible for others to speak up.

If this sounds familiar, it's because it is. In a world full of rampant misogyny, coming forward about having been sexually harassed or assaulted is often a harrowing prospect. Victims face intimidation, having to relive traumatic experiences, the unlikelihood of justice, and ridicule from the public, who may call them liars or gold diggers or worse. The result is that many survivors would rather keep silent.

But when one woman shares her story about an abusive man—especially when that man is in a position of power—it often breaks the dam, allowing others the accused has preyed upon to feel safer coming forward. These women are not riding a wave for 15 minutes of fame; they are emboldened and empowered by the examples of other victims. They see that they are not alone. They hope people will believe them. They are finding strength and safety in numbers.

"When one woman breaks the silence, others are empowered to tell their [stories]," Sonia Ossorio, president of the National Organization for Women—New York, an advocacy organization defending reproductive rights, fighting economic inequality, and aiming to end discrimination and violence against women and girls, tells *SELF*. "Together those stories paint the full picture and create an environment where victims are more likely to be believed."

Many of the Women Saying Weinstein Assaulted or Harassed Them Were Too Scared to Share Their Stories Publicly—Until Now.

The *New York Times'* October 5 exposé claimed that Weinstein has systematically sexually harassed and assaulted women for decades and paid many of them to keep silent. Since these first allegations broke, numerous other women have come forward saying that Weinstein harassed, assaulted, or raped them—and they had been too scared to say anything until now. Further coverage alleges that Weinstein's behavior was an "open secret" in Hollywood, and that previous stories about Weinstein's behavior may have been buried by powerful celebrities and politicians.

So far, at least 27 women have gone on the record about alleged harassment or assault from Weinstein, and many more have spoken out anonymously. Ashley Judd, who went on record for the *Times*, claimed that Weinstein invited her to have breakfast with him at a hotel. When she arrived, she said, he called her up to his suite and asked her for a massage, a shoulder rub, and to watch him shower. "I said no, a lot of ways, a lot of times, and he always came back at me with some new ask," she said. "It was all this bargaining, this coercive bargaining."

Since that story broke, other big names in Hollywood have revealed their own stories. Earlier this week, both Gwyneth Paltrow and Angelina Jolie shared that they, too, had been harassed by Weinstein. Jolie told the *Times* in an email, "I had a bad experience with Harvey Weinstein in my youth, and as a result, chose never to work with him again and warn others when they did. This behavior towards women in any field, any country is unacceptable." Paltrow says Weinstein invited her to a business meeting that turned out to be in his hotel suite, where he tried to massage her and invited her into his bedroom.

Other stories, detailed in the *Times* and in a separate investigative story in the *New Yorker*, include harrowing allegations of physical and psychological intimidation, assault, and rape.

People who report being assaulted face intense scrutiny, public disbelief, and attacks on their character. Critics have used the fact that many of Weinstein's accusers say he harassed them years or even decades ago to argue that the assaults did not happen or "weren't that bad." Along with a barrage of your typical Twitter trolls, fashion designer Donna Karan insinuated that women may be "asking for it" based on how they dress. (She has since apologized and claimed her comments were "misinterpreted.") Director Oliver Stone at first casted doubt on Weinstein's accusers, saying he would not "comment on gossip" and that Weinstein "shouldn't be condemned by a vigilante system." As the allegations mounted, he recanted, saying, "I've been traveling for the last couple of days and wasn't aware of all the women who came out to support the original story in the *New York Times*. After looking at what has been reported in many publications over the last couple of days, I'm appalled and commend the courage of the women who've stepped forward to report sexual abuse or rape."

"A major reason why survivors don't speak up is that they are afraid nothing will be done or they won't be believed. Too often they're met with questions that immediately place the doubt on them," Ossorio says. "As a society, we need to stop offering up doubt as the first response and start with believing."

Many of Weinstein's accusers report feeling isolated, scared that no one would believe them, and worried that coming forward would torpedo their careers. For victims afraid to come forward, knowing someone else has broken the silence before you step into such a harsh and unforgiving spotlight is invaluable.

In the Last Few Years Alone, We Have Seen Numerous Examples of Women Coming Forward En Masse Against an Alleged Harasser.

"We can see that there is a shift underway in public attitudes toward sexual assault and sexual harassment," Ossorio says. "We hope this is a turning point and one that sends a message to powerful men that they can no longer get away with sexual harassment." As she notes, the Weinstein allegations are just the latest example of many women sharing their stories after someone has broken the silence.

After comedian Hannibal Burres called Bill Cosby a rapist on stage in October 2014, scores of women came out accusing Cosby of sexual assault, drug-facilitated sexual assault, and rape. While five women had already spoken openly about Cosby allegedly assaulting them, the majority of his accusers came forward between November 2014 and August 2015, sometimes sharing their stories at the same press conferences.

At least 15 women have accused President Donald Trump of sexual assault, reporting incidents between the 1980s and 2013. These accusations were covered extensively in the media in October 2016, after a tape emerged in which Trump claimed you can "grab" women "by the pussy" as long as "you're a star." Trump was elected president of the United States one month later.

It doesn't even have to be against the same man; when Taylor Swift bravely testified against a DJ who groped her in 2013, calls to the Rape, Abuse & Incest National Network's hotline increased by 35 percent in just a few days. Reports of discrimination and sexual harassment in Silicon Valley have been emerging on a semi-regular basis since Ellen Pao filed a gender discrimination suit against her former employer Kleiner Perkins in 2012.

Whenever these kinds of stories come out, people question the women who have made accusations, claiming that they have invented these stories in order to get attention, money, or revenge. It's hard to argue as eerily similar accounts of harassment and assault emerge—and yet it happens anyway.

In a Case Like Weinstein's, There Is Clearly Comfort in Knowing You're Not Alone.

Regardless of what everyone else says, the women coming forward know for sure that Weinstein's other accusers will believe them—and that can mean everything.

It's completely understandable that these women feared the thought of standing up alone to a seemingly indestructible member of the Hollywood elite. And that it's only now, when so many others are speaking about their experiences, that they feel safe sharing their stories—and daring to hope that justice might be served (or at least future victims spared).

"There are more people willing to come forward now," Anita Hill, an attorney and civil rights advocate who accused Supreme Court Justice Clarence Thomas of sexual harassment, told *Variety* in an article about the Weinstein allegations. "There's obviously strength in numbers."

EVALUATING THE AUTHOR'S ARGUMENTS:

In this viewpoint, Nina Bahadur notes that victims of sexual assault and harassment may be afraid to speak up. Is the viewpoint convincing in its claim that victims should be believed, so all victims feel safe speaking up against their accusers? Why or why not?

One False Accusation Can Destroy Someone's Life

Benjamin Radford

"When you don't have to pay the consequences of your accusation it's easy to dismiss or minimize the damage done to an innocent person."

In the following excerpted viewpoint, Benjamin Radford begins by considering a case where a woman falsely accused a man of sexual assault. The author then lists several other cases of false accusations for sexual assault. He notes that most accusations are true, but a small percentage may be false. When someone is wrongly accused of a crime, the effects can be severe and long-lasting, even if that person is never convicted. Benjamin Radford is the deputy editor of Skeptical Inquirer, a journal published by the Center for Inquiry, which investigates controversial claims through science.

AS YOU READ, CONSIDER THE FOLLOWING QUESTIONS:
1. Why is it easier to prove that something did happen than to prove something did not happen?
2. Why might a person make a false accusation, according to the author?
3. What could happen to someone falsely accused of sexual assault, if they are convicted?

"The Anatomy of False Accusations: A Skeptical Case Study," by Benjamin Radford, Center for Inquiry, February 26, 2014. Reprinted by permission.

The accused deserve due process against claims of sexual misconduct. Despite evidence that most victims are truthful, a small percentage admit to fabricating their stories.

Robin Levitski, an eighteen-year-old student at Clarke University, told police in late 2013 that she had been abducted and sexually assaulted by a man she had met online several months earlier, and who she had dated.

[…]

It was a he-said / she-said story—except that the accused man had photographs of their encounter, taken during what Levitski described as a sexual assault. The photos provided independent documentary evidence of what happened between the two of them behind closed doors. The police officer accessed John's cell phone and "recovered images depicting sexual acts between John and Levitski." The police officer, however, immediately detected a problem: "The time date stamp on these images however was October 27 and Levitski could be seen smiling while lying next to John in one photo." Why would a woman be seen smiling next to a man who was sexually assaulting her, and why did the information in the photograph file indicate that the photos were taken on a different date than Levitski claimed?

[…]

Police "then presented Levitski with the evidence that they had uncovered which was contrary to her statements. After maintaining that she was telling the truth for approximately thirty minutes Levitski finally admitted that the entire story was fabricated to act as some sort of cover for the images that her grandmother had located on her cell phone. These images being of her and John engaged in sex acts. Levitski admitted that these photos were taken during a consensual sexual encounter between her and John on a date later than October 23, contrary to what she had reported."

A Closer Look

This case is fascinating and offers insight into the rarely-discussed dynamics of a demonstrably false report of abduction and sexual assault. This is not a case in which the circumstances are ambiguous, or authorities concluded that there was insufficient evidence to establish the accused person's guilt. This is an open-and-shut case in which all of the evidence, including the alleged victim's statements, clearly demonstrate that the accusation was false.

It also provides insight into how easy it is to make a claim, and how difficult it can be to disprove it. It took Levitski only a few minutes to make her claim to her grandmother, and then perhaps an hour to repeat the accusation to police. Investigators, however, spent many days on the case conducting multiple interviews, researching phone records, analyzing key entry data, and so on. This is as it should be: a thorough investigation into a young woman's serious accusations and a young man's life and liberty were on the line. But it does demonstrate the gross imbalance between the time and effort it takes to make a claim and the time and effort it takes to prove or disprove it. It is much easier to prove that something did happen (a positive claim) than to prove that something did not happen (proving a negative). False reports drain an enormous amount of time and money on police departments—time and money that could have been spent on investigating real crimes, with real victims.

[...]

Why Make a False Accusation?

Why would a person make it up? Only a person with a truly blinkered moral compass would even think of using a false accusation—much less one as serious as sexual assault—as a tool of revenge or convenient excuse for engaging in consensual sex. There is only one circumstance in which an accusation of sexual assault is appropriate: in the case of a genuine sexual assault. Not as a way to get back at someone you're upset with for other reasons. Not as a way to explain away embarrassing photos to your grandmother. False accusations are also a slap in the face to real victims of sexual assault.

Actually, Levitski's reason is mundane and common: the false report of a sexual assault is often used as cover story for consenting (but illicit) sexual activity. There are any number of reasons why a person might falsely claim to have been sexually assaulted, including revenge, seeking sympathy or attention, or to cover up for some crime, indiscretion, or infraction. Here's a few examples.

In 2007 a thirteen-year-old North Carolina girl told police that she had been abducted from her school bus stop by four Hispanic men in a dark red Ford Explorer, taken to nearby woods, and raped. Police canvassed the neighborhood but found nothing, and no eyewitnesses saw the incident. A medical exam revealed no evidence of any assault. Eventually the girl admitted that she had lied about the abduction and assault because she didn't want to get in trouble for skipping school.

On January 22, 2014, a twelve-year-old girl reported that she was approached by a white male as she was walking home from school; she said the man grabbed her and pulled down her pants before she was able to get away. Police searched the area but found no evidence that anything happened; the following day the girl confessed that she had not been assaulted at all; she had made up the story because she didn't want to get into trouble for missing her school bus. She is fortunate that an innocent man who happened to be in the area and who matched her general description was not pulled over and arrested on suspicion of attempted sexual assault.

[...]

Then there's the tragic case of Darrell Roberson, a Texas man who arrived at his home to find his wife Tracy underneath another man in the back of a pickup truck in their driveway. Tracy Roberson cried that she was being raped, upon which Mr. Roberson pulled out a gun and killed the other man with a shot to the head. It was soon determined that Tracy Roberson and the dead man, Devin LaSalle, had been caught in the middle of a consensual sexual affair. Though most cases do not result in anyone's death, false accusations of sexual assault often stem from an attempt to hide sexual infidelity from a partner.

What these cases have in common is that the person making the false report did not think through the consequences of their accusations. In fact this is a recurring theme in false claims of many serious crimes, including carjackings, robberies, school shootings, and even sexual assaults and kidnappings. When asked by police or reporters why a person made false report of a crime, typical responses are "I didn't realize it would be that big a deal" or "I didn't think it would get this far."

[...]

The Consequences

What are those consequences? Perhaps the most chilling aspect of this case is Levitski's utter indifference to the consequences of her claims for the man she recently dated. John might have been convicted of Sexual Abuse in the Second Degree (Iowa Code §709.3), which as a class B felony would have been punishable by up to 25 years in prison; or Sexual Abuse in the Third Degree (Iowa Code §709.4), which as a class C felony would be punishable by up to 10 years in prison and a fine of between $1,000 and $10,000. On abduction charge, he could have faced Kidnapping in the First Degree ("when the person kidnapped...is intentionally subjected to torture or sexual abuse"), which is a Class A felony and is punishable by life imprisonment (Iowa Code §902.9).

His family, friends, co-workers, and others find out, through rumor, gossip, and the local news, that he was arrested for abducting and sexually assaulting a young college woman. His name and mug shot in the local newspaper and on web sites, easily available to anyone with internet access. Once John is arrested he may be disenrolled and banned from campus by the university; what administration needs the negative publicity of allowing a man accused of abducting and raping another student back on their campus?

He loses his job when he goes to prison, if not long before during his arrest and trial. If he is married or has a family, he may lose them too. He and his family may have to pay tens (or hundreds) of thousands of dollars in legal fees to defend him—and why wouldn't they? Who wouldn't spend all they have to avoid a conviction and prison time for a crime they did not commit? These legal fees, of course, are non-refundable; even if he was found not guilty, he and his family may be left bankrupt by the accusations. His friends view him with suspicion: in their eyes he is a rapist—human garbage only a step or two removed from murderers and child molesters. John will be subject to the stress and dangers of prison life, possibly including rape or murder.

Because of his conviction and after he has served his "several years" for something he didn't do, he will have to register as a sex offender for years or possibly the rest of his life. Anyone who calls the local police station or looks online can find his name and address, and see that he served a prison sentence for abduction and rape. Think of how you would react if you found that information out about your next door neighbor, how you would treat him from then on, what you might say to warn other neighbors or visiting friends, about the predator next door. That (and much worse) is the reality of what "several years" in prison means. When you don't have to pay—or even think about—the consequences of your accusation it's easy to dismiss or minimize the damage done to an innocent person.

It's also easy to assume that Levitski's accusations are less serious because the case against the man never would have gone to trial, or that he never would have been convicted. However such faith in the justice system rests on shaky ground; the fact is that innocent men and women have been convicted of serious crimes on the basis of little more than the alleged victim's word. While it is likely that the man Levitsky accused would not have been indicted or convicted, it is far from a certainty—especially if he is poor or underprivileged and must rely on a public defender.

[...]

Why We Believe the "Victim"

Not just John and Robin's lives have been affected by her lies. What of those who rallied behind Robin Levitski, her family and friends who consoled her and supported her during the investigation, and those who joined her in accusing John? They of course had no reason to doubt Levitski's claims—why in the world would she make it up if it wasn't true?

[...]

Of course, most reports of sexual assault, abduction, and other serious crimes are true. The vast majority of the time when a man says he was carjacked, or a woman says she was assaulted, it really did happen. No one doubts or denies that, and that is part of the reason that victims are believed—as they should be, unless further evidence and investigation reveals that it did not happen. As Alan Dershowitz pointed out during a recent appearance on BBC News, most people who are accused of a crime are in fact guilty. We would not want to live in a world where most people, or even half of the people, who are accused of, or arrested for, a crime were innocent. We give lip service to the presumption of innocence of the accused, but the simple fact that someone in a position of authority took a claim seriously enough to investigate it suggests to many reasonable people there is likely some basis to it.

[...]

Saul Kassin, a social psychologist who appears in the documentary film *The Central Park Five*, explains why it is often very difficult for people to change their minds once they have decided that a person is guilty: "The problem is that once you form a strong belief that someone is guilty of a crime, the contradicting details are just that: they are details that don't fundamentally change our belief in their guilt."

[...]

Public Shame Is a Powerful Weapon

Ashwini Tambe

"By speaking publicly and shaming their harassers, victims have disrupted legal channels of redressal."

In the following viewpoint, Ashwini Tambe discusses the disruptive effect of the #MeToo movement. She notes that victims of sexual harassment are using social media to pursue justice, instead of legal channels. This allows them to bring attention to complaints that they might not be able to prove in a court of law. She notes that publicly shaming an attacker works better in certain fields, such as the media and politics. In those fields, people depend on their reputations. On the other hand, public shame is a weak weapon in many fields where women are harassed. Ashwini Tambe is Associate Professor in the Department of Women's Studies at the University of Maryland.

AS YOU READ, CONSIDER THE FOLLOWING QUESTIONS:
1. Why does the author call the #MeToo movement a "disruption"?
2. What is a disruptor, in the author's view?
3. Why are sexual harassment complaints more effective in some sectors than others?

Senator Al Franken gave in to pressure from his own party and stepped down from his position after a woman accused him of groping her a decade earlier.

Roy Moore's electoral defeat in Alabama is an important victory for #MeToo.

Let's recall that the allegations about his preying on teenagers came to light amidst a wave of #MeToo-inspired charges. National attention to sexual harassment raised the profile of this state-level race.

The focus has now turned to Donald Trump, as some members of Congress call for investigating multiple complaints of sexual misconduct against him. If their call gains traction, it will be a remarkable development.

The words "movement," "uprising," and even "revolution" have been used to describe events over the past two months. As a feminist scholar, I see them as apt because of the unprecedented momentum and scale of the outcry.

There is also another term that quite precisely conveys what is happening: "disruption." I borrow this term from technology and business writers who use it to describe an upheaval of institutionalized

ways of doing things. In many ways, what we are seeing is a textbook case of cultural disruption.

Moving "Relentlessly Upwards"

According to the theory, disruptors are typically small actors who ask: Why should we do things the same way as before? They offer new and low-cost solutions to problems from below, moving "relentlessly upwards" and "eventually displacing" established institutions. In our time, disruptions in the business world are mostly made possible by digital technology, the best examples being Netflix, which used digital streaming to subvert network television, and Airbnb, which directly connected home sharers with potential guests.

I see sexual harassment victims as disruptors because they use social media platforms to circumvent legal channels for pursuing justice. The current sea change began with little-known individuals using Twitter and Facebook to share personal stories, echoing the "survivor speak-out" model long championed by feminists of the anti-violence movement.

Short-Circuiting the Law

The scale of the viral #MeToo hashtag led journalists to investigate and publicize victims' stories. Effectively, this allowed a short-circuiting of the law. Lawsuits pose burdens of proof that are sometimes impossible to meet. How do you produce material evidence of unwanted touching or obscene words said in passing? So victims said: I need a different route to justice. By speaking publicly and shaming their harassers, victims have disrupted legal channels of redressal.

In court, you are innocent until proven guilty. But #MeToo has tilted public sympathy and power in favor of accusers by showing how widespread sexual coercion is. Taking accusers more seriously than those accused is a reversal of the principle of legal due process. Yet because those who are victimized have been so ill-served by legal burdens of proof, they are using the most effective alternative available. And many in the public are, for now, trusting the investigation process followed by reporters and management and ethics committees.

Some journalism outlets such as *The Washington Post* are using stringent investigative methods. Its reporters were not duped by false claims made by a sting operation. The pressure to be thorough and fair is very high, since the possibility of false accusations is real. This chaotic quality and the need for vigilance is reminiscent of other disrupted environments: Airbnb offers guests no guarantee of safety, and guests take on the risk of racism and sexual assault.

What remains to be worked out, after the dust settles, is a genuinely transformative solution to the problem of sexual coercion—one that goes beyond shaming and punishment to enabling perpetrators to take responsibility for the harm they have caused.

Targeting Specific Sectors

In the business world, disruptors typically take advantage of vulnerabilities in an industry or market. In this case, sexual harassment complaints are primarily effective in sectors where reputations matter, such as entertainment and politics. Media companies and political parties do not want to risk the public relations fallout from scandals. As a result, we see swift firings and resignations on the heels of allegations.

Yet media industries and politics, while being challenging environments for women, are not known to be the worst sites of gender-based abuse. The arenas considered historically unfriendly to women are male-dominated sectors such as construction and blue-collar trades, surgery and finance. The most troubling sectors, feminist scholars note, are those where private settings make abuse easier, such as domestic work or childcare, and service industries such as restaurants, where the pressure to seek tips make servers succumb to customer requests. But harassers in these sectors are not celebrities and therefore less vulnerable to public shaming.

The term "disruption" is also apt because it is a wholesale attack on an institution. Disruptors draw few distinctions between the valuable and less-valuable features of institutions, or the worst or least offensive perpetrators. The goal is to upend a system, or in this case, to root out a systematic problem. For instance, the distinctions between Democrat and Republican party positions on women's issues seem less meaningful right now, as allegations against members of both parties spill out. The pent-up fury driving victims to come forward has meant dispensing with this distinction.

Finally, it is worth noting that the energy associated with this movement, as with many disruptors, is youthful. The driving force behind the movement against sexual harassment is young women, who, according to a Pew survey, most readily identify it as a widespread problem. This is not surprising; it is those in the age range of 15-35 years who are most frequently harassed, and the young are also the most avid users of social media platforms. Women in older age groups are, of course, also speaking out about past experiences of harassment and its very real effect on their lives and careers. But in the impatience and refusal of the status quo, we can distinctly hear a new generation's voice.

EVALUATING THE AUTHOR'S ARGUMENTS:

In this viewpoint, Ashwini Tambe notes that some victims of sexual harassment are using social media to accuse their victims. What are the pros and cons of this method rather than using legal channels? Is the ability to publicly shame someone a good or bad thing, in the author's view? How do you feel about it? Would you feel differently if you hadn't read the concerns in the previous viewpoint?

Beware of the "Chilling Effect"

Patrice Lee Onwuka

"Policies intended to help women in the workforce led to smaller paychecks and fewer opportunities."

In the following viewpoint, Patrice Lee Onwuka discusses the potential "chilling effect" caused by fear of sexual harassment accusations. A chilling effect happens when people are afraid to say or do things that are legal, out of fear of negative results. When it comes to accusations of sexual harassment, this fear could lead to a backlash against women. For example, a man may not want to hire female employees for fear that they may accuse him of sexual harassment if they misinterpret his innocent words or actions. Patrice Lee Onwuka is a senior policy analyst at Independent Women's Forum.

AS YOU READ, CONSIDER THE FOLLOWING QUESTIONS:

1. How could men's fear of sexual harassment accusations make it harder for women to get jobs and promotions?
2. How does mentoring typically happen, according to the viewpoint?
3. Should companies hire more or fewer women, according to the author?

"Sheryl Sandberg Calls Out the Chilling Effect Between Sexes Following Harassment Revelations," by Patrice Lee Onwuka, Senior Policy Analyst, Independent Women's Forum, December 5, 2017. Reprinted by permission.

A potential reaction to the #MeToo movement might be lack of opportunity and willingness for men to interact with women in the workplace, which would be detrimental to the career development and success of women.

Sheryl Sandberg penned an essay on Facebook this weekend with her thoughts about sexual harassment in the workplace and how to turn this "watershed moment" into positive change.

While she regurgitated some of the pervasive victim narrative, she rightly called out the chilling effect on interactions between men and (younger) women today as well as the unintended consequences to women's career advancement when we paint all men as monsters.

As a leading woman in business and technology, the 48-year-old *Lean In* author and Facebook COO is looked to as a mentor to women in the workplace. Women will eat up her advice the way women took Oprah's words as gospel in the 1990s.

What does Sandberg say about how we can use this time of reckoning to address and stop sexual harassment? First, she positions sexual harassment—like sexual assault—as an issue of power at its core. So empowering victims to speak up and for the perpetrators to be held responsible is important. She cautions though that there is reason to worry about backlash against women in the workplace:

> *I have already heard the rumblings of a backlash: "This is why you shouldn't hire women." Actually, this is why you should.*
>
> *And you shouldn't just hire women—you should mentor, advise, and promote them.*

According to Sandberg data already revealed this chilling effect was in operation well before the wave of #MeToo allegations this year:

> *Four years ago, I wrote in Lean In that 64 percent of senior male managers were afraid to be alone with a female colleague, in part because of fears of being accused of sexual harassment. The problem with this is that mentoring almost always occurs in one-on-one settings...*

We can only imagine how those numbers have changed since then. The natural reaction for many men—including those who do respect women—may be to pull back on their one-on-one interactions with junior female colleagues. That is exactly what women don't need Sandberg says:

> *Doing right by women in the workplace does not just mean treating them with respect. It also means not isolating or ignoring them—and making access equal. Whether that means you take all your direct reports out to dinner or none of them, the key is to give men and women equal opportunities to succeed. This is a critical moment to remind ourselves how important this is. So much good is happening to fix workplaces right now. Let's make sure it does not have the unintended consequence of holding women back.*

Sandberg is right about unintended consequences. As we've seen, policies intended to help women in the workforce such as paid leave mandates led to smaller paychecks and fewer opportunities, especially for younger women. For example, when we look at European countries, which have generous mandated paid leave benefits studies, we find that fewer women are in managerial positions compared to American women and more women were working part-time and in lower paid jobs.

American women comprise 47 percent of the labor force, and we are not going anywhere anytime soon. However, there are still more men in the labor force and in leadership or influential roles than women and they play critical roles. They are allies, advocates, mentors, coaches, sponsors, advisors, and partners to women.

As Sandberg notes, coaching opportunities often occur in one-on-one settings. What we don't need is for men to feel afraid to be alone with a woman. That is the by-product of a national conversation that inadvertently begins to demonize all men.

Sandberg pushes for more women in senior roles as a solution. That's a welcome goal. However, those pushing for parity need to be more realistic.

Many women are choosing not to climb the ladder, not because of systemic sexism, but because they may not want senior roles which often carry demanding schedules like constant travel. Many women would trade higher pay and promotions for greater flexibility in their jobs to care for an aging parent or to raise a family. Workplaces are increasingly recognizing the value workers place on flexible arrangements (such as telework, compressed schedules, and job-sharing) and retooling to offer what is good for their workers. This is a good thing.

Sexual harassment is intolerable and unjustifiable. Now, is a critical time to hear from the victims who come forward, to punish wrong-doing and to reintroduce greater respect for women (and men) in the workplace.

As society pursues truth and justice in addressing sexual harassment, we must do so in a way that doesn't paint all men as predators and all women as victims. The consequences could set us all back.

EVALUATING THE AUTHOR'S ARGUMENTS:

In this viewpoint, Patrice Lee Onwuka warns about a potential side effect to accusations of sexual harassment in the workplace. A "chilling effect" could cause women to miss more job opportunities. What does the author conclude is the proper way to handle this concern? Do you agree or disagree?

Viewpoint

5

Is the Patriarchy at an End?

Emine Saner

"It is beginning to look as if not a single industry will escape allegations of sexual harassment."

In the following viewpoint, Emine Saner discusses how accusations of sexual harassment have spread from Hollywood to other fields. Men have lost jobs in media, theater, fashion, politics, and even charity organizations due to sexual harassment accusations, leading some to believe this signals a major attack on the patriarchy and may topple societies where men hold the power. Others worry that things will return to the way they were in the past. The author quotes several women and their opinions on whether the current movement will effect long-term change in society. Emine Saner is a feature writer for the *Guardian*.

AS YOU READ, CONSIDER THE FOLLOWING QUESTIONS:

1. How are accusations from privileged women often treated differently from those by poor and minority women?
2. How do some men enable others to commit sexual harassment and assaults?
3. What needs to happen in order to create real change, according to the author?

"Women and Men Are Speaking Out about Abuse – Is This the End of the Patriarchy?" by Emine Saner, Guardian News and Media Limited, October 30, 2017. Reprinted by permission.

Caught up in the momentum of what seems like a turning point for women, activists and political leaders organized marches and conventions to focus on action.

I t is beginning to look as if not a single industry will escape allegations of sexual harassment—something that will not, of course, come as a surprise to most working women. The explosive allegations of sexual assault by the film producer Harvey Weinstein, spanning several decades, have become a huge talking point because his victims are well-known names. And this has led to an outpouring, in Hollywood and far beyond.

At the weekend, Vicky Featherstone, artistic director of the Royal Court, held a "day of action," which included a stage reading, lasting over five hours, of more than 150 testimonies of sexual harassment within the theatre industry; she is now drawing up an industry code of conduct. The director Max Stafford-Clark was forced out of his theatre company, Out of Joint, after young female colleagues reported sexual comments he had made to them ("Back in the day, I'd have been up you like a rat up a drainpipe," he allegedly said to one female employee, in her 20s at the time). When this emerged, actor Tracy Ann Oberman wrote she had a "sense that chickens were coming home to roost in this post-Weinstein world," detailing her own humiliating and upsetting experiences with Stafford-Clark 25 years ago.

At the BBC, a Five Live commentator has been suspended over a sexual harassment claim, and another broadcaster is being investigated. Within the art world, 2,000 people, including artists, curators and museum directors, signed a letter in protest against sexual harassment, in the wake of the resignation last week of an influential art publisher who had been subject to accusations. The charity Oxfam is investigating allegations of sexual harassment and exploitation, with one director having already been dismissed.

The fashion world, which up until now has largely ignored the shocking, detailed reports made by models about the behaviour of photographer Terry Richardson, suddenly decided he was not to be trusted any more—a leaked email from publishing giant Condé Nast said he should no longer be employed by their magazines, including *Vogue*. Women within the music industry have started speaking out about sexual assault and harassment, too.

Stories about senior politicians, running from sexual assault and blackmail to inappropriate "jokes," have emerged, and yesterday the Labour MP Tulip Siddiq said the number of cases could run into "the hundreds". This has "gone past gossip" she told the BBC, "this is a serious problem".

This isn't something perpetrated only by men against women; in situations where there has been a clear power differential, men and boys have been victims, too. James Van Der Beek wrote on Twitter about his experiences as a young actor with "older, powerful men … there's a power dynamic that feels impossible to overcome." The actor and former NFL player Terry Crews also wrote on Twitter, in the wake of the Weinstein allegations, that he had been assaulted by an unnamed Hollywood executive. And actor Anthony Rapp alleged that Kevin Spacey had made sexual advances towards him when he was just 14. Spacey responded that he didn't remember the encounter, "But if I did behave then as he describes, I owe him the sincerest apology for what would have been deeply inappropriate drunken behaviour."

There has been an outpouring, an unravelling, stories shared on WhatsApp groups, urgent whispers in corridors, rumours becoming allegations. Have we been here before or does all this feel different? Is it, as Naomi Wolf wrote this month, a "rend in the fabric of patriarchy"? Featherstone echoed this phrase, saying she feels optimistic that we have reached a point of no return, "we have got to the top of a mountain, and a rip has been torn in the patriarchy. I'm not saying it will all be solved, but things will never be the same again."

"What worries me is how quickly things return to normal," says the writer and activist Joan Smith. "We have been in similar situations in the past. I'm just hoping that this time—because it's not just limited to one institution—it's spreading out much more widely and it might actually be a watershed."

We have been here before—Savile, Rochdale, Rotherham and other gross acts of abuse against some of the most vulnerable people —and the world hasn't noticeably changed, has it? "Absolutely," says Joanna Bourke, professor of history at Birkbeck College and author of *Rape: A History from 1860 to the Present*. "Feminists have been fighting this issue ever since feminism began. You can see it before the 18th century, but certainly from the 18th century onwards sexual violence and harassment have been really big [issues] for women. I do think however that there have been major changes and improvements, especially in law in terms of what is appropriate. I don't think patriarchy is going to end but it is an important point—the ability and the increasing willingness to go public is really important because one of the problems we always have when it comes to these issues are the aspects of shame and [the idea that] somehow the person who is affected by it is somehow responsible. The fact that more people are talking about it is a fantastic turning point."

However, she adds, "one of the reasons why there is a discussion about it is because the women who have come forward are influential, believable, well-known and privileged, in terms of class and status. It still remains formidably difficult for minority groups, poor women, women who are regarded or believed to be less attractive than others to come forward and talk about these things."

The campaigner Nimco Ali, co-founder of the Daughters of Eve project, says perhaps the reason it feels different this time is "it has happened to white, well-known women [and] people are taking note. I think that's the thing—if it happened to that person then it must be true. Jimmy Savile had power and people covered up for him; in the Rotherham case, nobody really cared about white working-class girls."

Photographs of attractive, famous women—Angelina Jolie, Gwyneth Paltrow, Cara Delevingne—have accompanied the Weinstein story. "Nobody would care if they were poor, unattractive women. It's selling newspapers and everybody else is reading it. I think it's quite depressing in that sense. I think the only reason we're talking about it is because it's in the press, and the only reason it's in the press is because attractive women are being sexualised again and again."

Ali says she hadn't even thought about it as the beginning of the end of patriarchy. "I think that's wishful thinking. Is it an impetus to do something? Maybe. It's [about] saying now it's come to the forefront, are we going to do something about it or are we going to sensationalise it?"

Pragna Patel, director of Southall Black Sisters, says this moment is certainly important. "The problem is not women coming forward but how institutions respond to that and we still have a long way to go in terms of ensuring there are the resources, including women's organisations that can effectively support women through quite trau-matic experiences. Many women's organisations are closing or facing closure due to cutbacks. I'm particularly concerned about black and minority women who live in some of the most marginalised, hard-to-reach communities, where sexual harassment and sexual violence is still very much taboo. They particularly need to come forward, but the specialist organisations for BAME women are closing at an alarm-ing rate due to lack of funds. So it's a really contradictory situation in which we find ourselves—a blow for patriarchy but it's not going to be the nail in the coffin until the state also gives commitment to providing the resources needed to ensure that when women come forward they are supported. Sadly, the culture of disbelief prevails in institutions, sexual violence and abuse is still trivialised and so we still have a long way to go."

She thinks it is significant that the outpouring has spread from the largely US-based entertainment industry, to Britain's theatre and art world, the BBC, charities and parliament; WhatsApp groups share stories of harassment in journalism, too. "It does feel like this is a really important moment that everyone who cares about the rights of women and girls should really grasp, and that means condemning such actions but also providing the resources to ensure that when women do finally come forward, they are actually helped in meaningful ways. It may well be a turning point in relation to the institutional culture of sexual harassment, but we cannot use this moment to create a culture of expectancy and then not meet needs."

In the US, a conversation about sexual harassment has gone on for more than a quarter of a century, bookended by two events. In 1991, Anita Hill—a law professor—testified before an all-male panel of senators after making allegations of sexual harassment against her former boss Clarence Thomas, who had been nominated to the supreme court. This young African-American woman spoke confidently and defiantly. Thomas denied the allegations and was confirmed to the supreme court that year. Hill was dismissed in public as a "scorned woman," and worse.

"What happened as a result of that was people began to talk about sexual harassment in a way they never had before," says Michael Kimmel, professor of sociology and gender studies at Stony Brook University. "My mother told me about being sexually harassed when she was in graduate school. Many people told their parents, their children, their partners that this had happened to them. These were private conversations, but nothing public because of the way [Hill] was treated."

Twenty-five years later, a 2005 tape emerged during the US presidential campaign in which Donald Trump boasted about sexually assaulting women. There was horror at his comments, but it ultimately didn't harm him—with 53% of white women voters opting for him. Last week, the White House press secretary was asked about the allegations of sexual misconduct against Trump by at least 16 women, and she reiterated Trump's view that it was "fake news," and that the women were lying.

"This time, it feels a little bit different," says Kimmel. "It feels like the women are being believed publicly, and women are lining up to talk about this. I think this is another moment in the long progression of the renegotiation of the relationship between women and men at work. This is about the entitlement felt by men in power that they can do these sorts of things. We've witnessed over the past 25 years the gradual believing of women when they tell these stories."

But the beginning of the end of patriarchy? Hardly, says Kimmel. "There is another element to this case. It's not simply the behaviour of these predatory, powerful men, it's also the enabling of them by other men. The key player in the Trump case was Billy Bush—had he said to Trump, 'That's disgusting, not to mention illegal', Trump would not have been so quick to brag about sexual assault … Yes, it's true that that sense of male entitlement may be eroding as these women come forward, but as long as that part of patriarchy continues—where some men enable other men—it will continue.

"We need to remember how long-term and embedded these problems are," says Bourke. "And how things change really slowly." Perhaps the immediacy and clamour of social media has fooled us into thinking we're at a tipping point, rather than something ephemeral that might burn out. Social media has been great for feminism, she says, and particularly in the context of sexual assault and harassment "because it has enabled people to get in touch and realise they're not alone. But in terms of a political response, that's not going far enough."

But then you look at an organisation such as Everyday Sexism and see the vast archive of sexual harassment women have endured. "I had absolutely no idea that it would snowball in the way that it has," says its founder Laura Bates. "What's happened, with several hundred thousand stories, has taken me completely by surprise." This recent outpouring of stories, she says, "is the most incredible show of solidarity, strength and collective action, but women alone sharing their stories don't have the power to change things. What really needs to change is men's behaviour and structural, systemic, organisational inequality."

This moment has the potential to be important, she says, but "I'd even be cautious about labelling this as a tipping point. What we've seen is incredible courage and strength on the part of many women, and some men, in coming forward and sharing their stories in an environment in which it's incredibly difficult to do so, and that has the potential to push it in the right direction, but whether it will or not depends on what happens next. What really matters is how we respond to the courage of those people who have come forward—do we tackle institutional and ingrained inequality, do we start as individuals challenging this behaviour instead of turning a blind eye, do organisations from businesses to schools and universities take this as the moment to put in place genuinely radical strategies for tackling this? Or do we all talk about it in the media, act shocked and appalled, and then wait a few weeks for it to die down and then go on exactly as we were before?"

EVALUATING THE AUTHOR'S ARGUMENTS:

In this viewpoint, Emine Saner quotes various sources discussing whether the current movement will end the patriarchy, and with that greatly reduce sexual harassment and assault. Does the viewpoint come to any conclusions on this matter?

Chapter 2

How and When Should We Punish People?

Punishment for criminal behavior is obvious, but for other degrees of misbehavior it's not so clear.

Viewpoint

1

Don't Support People Who Do Bad Things

Lauren Porosoff

"How do we respond when we discover that someone we look up to is not at all the person we thought?"

In the following viewpoint, Lauren Porosoff discusses accusations against Sherman Alexie, a popular author of books for young people. The viewpoint author had been using one of Alexie's books in the classroom with great results. Then a number of women accused Alexie of sexual harassment. He admitted fault in some cases and denied other accusations. The viewpoint author decided to stop teaching Alexie's book. Instead she will seek out other books that support marginalized and disadvantaged authors. Still, she grieves over the loss of an author she admired and a book she found useful in the classroom. Lauren Porosoff is a sixth-grade English teacher in New York.

AS YOU READ, CONSIDER THE FOLLOWING QUESTIONS:

1. How did Sherman Alexie's behavior hurt the careers of First Nation women writers, according to the viewpoint?
2. How is this a teachable moment, according to the author?
3. How could these accusations affect the students reading Alexie's book?

"Why I'll Never Teach This Powerful Book Again," by Lauren Porosoff, Teaching Tolerance, March 2, 2018. Reprinted with permission of Teaching Tolerance, a project of the Southern Poverty Law Center. https://www.tolerance.org/magazine/why-ill-never-teach-this-powerful-book-again.

Inspired by the brave confessions of others, many women—and men—are speaking up about their own experiences. This has derailed the careers and tarnished the legacies of many men, but the effects can be even further reaching.

This week I heard the news, which in some communities wasn't news at all, that author Sherman Alexie has been accused by multiple women of sexual harassment, intimidation and humiliation.

My sixth-grade English classes were right in the middle of our unit on *The Absolutely True Diary of a Part-Time Indian*. The book is an illustrated first-person narrative from the point of view of 14-year-old Arnold Spirit Jr., who leaves the Spokane Reservation to attend a school in a nearby white town. *True Diary* has provided a vehicle for us to discuss intersecting identities. For example, students make lists of Arnold's identifiers (Spokane, male, 14 years old) and use these to create questions like: What does it mean for Arnold to be both ____ and ____? (For example, Spokane and male?) How has Arnold discovered new ways of being ____? What does being ____ give Arnold access to? What does being ____ limit Arnold's access to?

At the end of the unit, each student writes and illustrates an "absolutely true" personal essay about their own intersecting identities. One girl wrote about being the product of artificial insemination. A boy wrote about how white girls didn't consider him dateable because he's black. Another boy wrote about the assumptions people make about him because he has ADHD. A student who later came out as nonbinary wrote about their experience of being forced to wear a dress. It's the kind of writing assignment where even the essays with grammatical or structural shortcomings are good because they're about topics that genuinely matter to the students, and their voices come through.

This unit has consistently spurred some of the deepest discussions and most powerful writing that students do in all of sixth grade and perhaps in all of middle school.

So I am furious with Sherman Alexie.

I'm furious, first and foremost, over what an untold number of First Nation women writers said he did. These are women whose work and names I don't know—in part because of my own ignorance and blind spots, in part because of institutional racism in the publishing industry and in part (if we believe them, and I do) because of Alexie's actions.

I'm furious that this is yet another "teachable moment" for us to process. While I do believe in using current events to foster a sense of responsibility to act for justice, discussing this event will take time away from noticing and choosing how they want to relate to their reading, their writing, each other, the world and themselves. My students will lose a writing day for this discussion.

And I'm furious that this will become a distraction from the important work this unit has elicited in the past. When students remember this unit, they might or might not remember the questions they wrote about intersecting identities (What does it mean to have a mom and no dad? What does it mean to be black at my school? What does it mean to be nonbinary in my family?). They might or might not remember the cartoons they drew, the thoughtful responses they wrote or the emotionally charged annotations they scrawled in their books as they tried to make their pens keep up with their brains.

But they will remember the accusations against the author whose book they loved.

The same day I heard the news, one of my school's diversity coordinators emailed me to make sure I knew. She asked what I planned to do. My grade-level partner and I decided—and our leadership and diversity teams agreed—that our school would stand by the women of the #MeToo movement and would not contribute to Alexie's popularity or bank account by teaching his book next year.

My partner and I immediately got to work on identifying a new text about intersectional identities that we could teach next year, focusing on First Nations authors. We ordered copies of Eric Gansworth's *If I Ever Get Out of Here* and Cynthia Leitich Smith's *Rain Is Not My Indian Name*. We also ordered the anthology *Open Mic: Riffs on Life Between Cultures in Ten Voices*, edited by Mitali Perkins, thinking these essays would serve as excellent models for our students' writing. Since we'd lose the parts of the *True Diary* unit in which students analyze the cartoons in the book and create their own, we talked about adding a graphic novel into the curriculum. We looked at graphic novels by women and authors of color: Cece Bell's *El Deafo*, Svetlana Chmakova's *Awkward*, and Mariko Tamaki and Jillian Tamaki's *This One Summer*. We're still not sure exactly how we'll fill the void *True Diary* will leave, but we're hopeful about the possibilities for next year.

What to do this year presents a more complicated problem. We won't ignore this important issue and want to teach into it: How do we respond when we discover that someone we look up to is not at all the person we thought? Is it ethical to appreciate a piece of work when the person who created it behaved wrongfully? We hope to discuss these questions after our classes finish the book so that we don't detract from their reading experience—although there's no telling whether the students will be as authentic or go as deep in their writing after learning about the allegations against Alexie.

In *True Diary*, when Junior is in the middle of his "grief-storm" over the deaths of his beloved grandmother and sister, he says that writing about his experiences became his grieving ceremony. This piece of writing is mine.

EVALUATING THE AUTHOR'S ARGUMENTS:

In this viewpoint, Lauren Porosoff decided to stop teaching Sherman Alexie's book after he was accused of sexual harassment. Is it fair to stop supporting an author by buying his books, if he is accused of sexual harassment? What are the advantages and disadvantages to doing so?

Lighten Up— It's Not Always Abuse

> *"This endless torrent of sexual harassment allegations makes it harder for truly harassed and abused women to get justice."*

Debra DeAngelo

In the following viewpoint, Debra DeAngelo opens by joking about men. She then shares her reactions to the sexual harassment accusations against actor Kevin Spacey. She asks if people have gone too far in punishing men accused of sexual harassment, without a legal trial and conviction. She suggests that the current climate is making half the population into villains, when sometimes their actions are not that bad. She suggests women need to lighten up while at the same time being willing to fight back when they do encounter harassment or rudeness. Debra DeAngelo is a columnist and editor who specializes in writing opinion and commentary pieces.

AS YOU READ, CONSIDER THE FOLLOWING QUESTIONS:
1. What is the difference between harassment and being crass, according to the author?
2. How can one judge when it's harassment versus "crassitude," according to the author?
3. What is the danger of giving equal weight to minor and major claims of sexual harassment, according to the author?

Is it possible for the public to reserve its opinion until all the facts are in? It is all too tempting to get caught up in the drama of initial accusations.

Apparently men can no longer be allowed in the workplace. Going forward, men will only be allowed as house pets. I keed, I keed…

Because, come on—men make crummy house pets. They're big, noisy and messy, and exceedingly difficult to leash-train. They'd do better as livestock—kept outside in a corral until haltered and led by an experienced handler.

Man Saddles!

I totally just copyrighted that, and this column is evidence. It's in print and dated. Don't mess with me, because I'll have at least one lawyer in my nifty little man stable.

Before your righteous indignation gets all in a bunch—exhale: I keed, I keed.

If you're offended by inappropriate or shocking banter, pal, you're reading the wrong column. I make no apologies. I am what I am. The chili pepper does not apologize for not tasting like strawberry ice cream.

Chili peppers gotta pepp.

You want sweetness and light, go watch kitten videos on YouTube.

Anyway.

The point here isn't whether I harbor sexist views about men (OK, I do, but that's still not the point)—the point is: Can we joke about anything anymore? If everything is so blasted serious, how will we know when something is actually harmful? Have we become haunted by our humorless Puritan ancestors?

When did we become so uptight? So thin-skinned and fragile, so hypersensitive and hypervigilant, that any whiff of sexuality propels us into sexual harassment hysteria, fleeing to the nearest authority to point the finger of damnation? Moreover, when did accusations become convictions? Back in the 1600s, women were convicted and sentenced to death for witchcraft simply because someone else claimed she was a witch. No proof, just accusations. Is it 1692 all over again?

I feel like I've tumbled into Bizarro World—down is up, up is down, and nothing makes sense, because be clear: I'm a feminist! I grew up in the shadow of Gloria Steinem and bra-burning and the (still infuriatingly unratified) Equal Rights Amendment. I have my Pink Pussy Hat and I ain't afraid to use it!

But amid this high-speed montage of sexual harassment, I had a tipping point: Kevin Spacey. I adore him. I'll watch a movie, even a junky one, just because he's in it. So when an allegation emerged from a then-underage person that Spacey hit on him while both were intoxicated at a Hollywood party three decades ago, and just like that, Spacey was bounced off his successful "House of Cards" series on Netflix, I had to pump the brakes.

Wait a minute… what was a minor doing at a drunken Hollywood celebrity party? Where were his parents? Did Spacey even know he was a minor? Hollywood isn't famed for propriety, let alone with cocktails. Maybe Spacey was behaving like a jerk, but contextually speaking, is this alleged assault really so shocking?

"Alleged."

What a precious little yester-year word.

Between the social media feeding frenzy and the regular media tossing bucket after bucket of tasty "gotcha" chum into the waters, there's no such thing as "allegation" anymore. Guilty! Send him to the stocks and tattoo a scarlet SH (Sexual Harasser) on his forehead.

Am I the only one clinging to the winsome notion of due process? Constitutional rights? A fair and speedy trial? Better question: Am I the only one worried about abandoning them?

This is where it gets all Bizarro World-y.

Women have irrefutably been discounted and blamed for their abuse at the hands of men, beginning with Eve herself. When Adam —who bit the apple of his own free will—was confronted by God, Adam declared "she made me do it" without missing a beat. That was good enough for God—The Man said it, so it must be true. Sadly, it's been this way for women ever since.

Women must be taken seriously when they're abused, harassed and raped. But there's a process: allegation, charges, evidence, trial, verdict. That's the very foundation of our society, and if we abandon it, our country is in danger of utter disintegration.

Take the allegations against Garrison Keillor. Garrison Keillor! The icon! Mr. *Prairie Home Companion*! An oasis of human goodness in an otherwise insane world!

In a follow-up Washington Post story, a befuddled Keillor said he didn't even know what the allegations were—his employer never even laid them all out—but suspected an incident when he touched a woman's bare back while trying to console her. She recoiled. He said he was sorry. That wasn't good enough. Sound the alarms! It's sexual assault! Especially if I'll get my moment on E!

Wow. "Touch" equals "assault"? I better stop hugging people before I'm accused of pre-rape. That will be next. "Pre-crimes." Maybe *Minority Report* was actually pre-reality.

Then there was another gal who came forward, claiming Al Franken groped her. While hugging her for a photo, she claims he grabbed her breast. Stephanie Kemplin, an Army veteran, recounted this story, misty-eyed and through tears of her trauma.

Give me a break.

First off, yes, people's hands sometimes land on a breast, unintentionally and to everyone's embarrassment. I've had it happen to me. I've even done it myself. What can you do but roll your eyes, particularly when the "offender" is horrified.

Second, if someone grabbed my breast, and I knew it was an intentional feel, whatever happened to ramming an elbow into his ribs? Kemplin was in the ARMY. She knew how to defend herself against this and far worse. And this "groping" was enough to traumatize her for 20 years?

Give me two breaks.

Seriously, people, where does it end? This lifelong feminist says enough's enough. Every juvenile, lunk-headed male comment, every whistle, every pat on the shoulder isn't sexual harassment. All men aren't bad. They're just not. Bad house pets, yes. But not intrinsically bad.

Vilifying half of the population isn't the answer to equality. Worse yet, this endless torrent of sexual harassment allegations, both egregious and microscopic but given equal weight, makes it harder for truly harassed and abused women to get justice. Their voices are lost in the roar.

We need a litmus test. If your boss says your promotion requires kneepads, that's harassment. If some random idiot says he'd like to see you on kneepads, that's not harassment. That's crassitude.

Yes, that's a word, and perfect for our current sexual harassment confusion. And oh, what serendipitous joy that "ass" is the core of both "harassment" and "crassitude," because that's the best label for men who demean women and treat them like boobs on legs.

Is it harassment or crassitude? Simple: If you give him a middle finger and a well-deserved verbal vivisection, will you get fired? No? It's crassitude. Did it happen at work? Yes? It's harassment.

Ladies, the world isn't our babysitter. It's not the world's job to take care not to rattle our tender sensitivities. If you go through life as a victim, all the world's an assailant. That said, whether crassitude or harassment, we need to confront it, fearlessly. But we need to know the difference. And also … we need to lighten up a little. Puritanism makes your butt look fat.

EVALUATING THE AUTHOR'S ARGUMENTS:

In this viewpoint, Debra DeAngelo suggests that some behavior is merely crass, not sexual harassment. Is this piece news reporting or personal opinion? How do the humor and the emotional tone of her writing support or detract from the author's claims?

Corporations Must Focus on Discrimination

Elizabeth C. Tippett

"This just-do-nothing ethos was a terrible judgement from a moral and public relations standpoint."

In the following viewpoint, Elizabeth C. Tippett explores how the #MeToo movement affected Nike, a company that makes sports apparel. Woman at the company grew tired of years of sexual harassment and gender discrimination. When Nike's human resources department did nothing, the women took their complaints public. This led to bad publicity for Nike, and some executives resigned. The author notes that there is a legal difference between harassment and discrimination. She suggests that stronger antidiscrimination policies would help companies know where to draw the line. Elizabeth C. Tippett is an Associate Professor at the University of Oregon School of Law.

AS YOU READ, CONSIDER THE FOLLOWING QUESTIONS:
1. What are "easy cases" and "hard cases" in law?
2. How severe must conduct be in order to be legally considered workplace harassment?
3. What is the difference between harassment and discrimination?

"Nike's #MeToo Moment Shows How 'Legal' Harassment Can Lead to Illegal Discrimination," by Elizabeth C. Tippett, The Conversation, May 1, 2018, https://theconversation.com/nikes-metoo-moment-shows-how-legal-harassment-can-lead-to-illegal-discrimination-95828. Licensed under CC BY ND 4.0.

Many corporate human resources departments would do well to focus on discrimination in the workplace rather than harassment. Because of legal loopholes, it's often too easy to get around claims of harrassment.

Nike's having its #MeToo moment—and it illustrates plainly what's still missing from our discussion of sexual harassment in the workplace.

Women at Nike, fed up with the status quo, recently undertook a covert survey asking about sexual harassment and gender discrimination, which eventually reached the CEO of the world's largest sports brand. Six top executives have resigned or announced their departure.

Nike employees interviewed by *The New York Times* described being marginalized and passed over for promotion. One recounted a supervisor that called her "stupid bitch." Another reported an email from a manager about an employee's breasts. There was the manager who bragged about condoms in his bag and racy magazines on his desk. Oh, and of course there were trips to strip clubs, tacked on to the end of staff outings.

This happened over a period of years. All the while, human resources sat on its hands. The managers kept their jobs. The complaints piled on.

In some ways, it's the familiar story of how companies have long turned a blind eye to harassment. But it also illustrates, perhaps better than any other example from the #MeToo era, how harassment can be a symptom—and precursor— of workplace discrimination.

And, as I explain in a forthcoming article in the *Minnesota Law Review*, understanding that link is critical for companies hoping to improve upon past mistakes.

Easy vs. Hard

The #MeToo movement has rightly brought attention to questions of sexual harassment and assault. The types of cases that result could be divided into two buckets—what in law school we would label "easy cases" and "hard cases."

One of the first thing students learn in law school is that "easy cases" refer to those in which the facts are really extreme—where a rule clearly applies or it doesn't. Here, that would mean egregious examples of sexual harassment, such as allegations of Matt Lauer's lewd and aggressive behavior toward subordinates.

"Hard cases" refer to situations where it's harder to figure out whether the parties involved have violated the rule. There might be arguments on both sides, and it might be hard to predict how a court would rule. Or—a favored trap on the bar exam—the conduct might seem really bad as a matter of common sense but doesn't meet the technical requirements of the legal rule.

The stories coming out of Nike are the hard cases. They do not clearly meet the legal standard for workplace harassment.

The Problem of Not-Quite Harassment

The law governing workplace harassment is quite unforgiving. The offensive conduct must be so severe or frequent that it creates an abusive working environment. The conduct must also be motivated by the victim's membership in a protected category, like their gender or race.

Some legal scholars have argued courts have been too unforgiving in applying this test and that it should be brought closer to common-sense understandings of harassment.

Lawyers and human resources experts have long known that the legal standard for harassment is incredibly high. So companies worked around it by defining harassment very broadly in their policies. This gave companies the power (but not the obligation) to punish employees for violations of the policy. But pre-#MeToo, it seemed companies chose not to act, even when they had the power to do so.

As we now know, this just-do-nothing ethos was a terrible judgment from a moral and public relations standpoint. And while companies may have been correct that a claim may not have been harassment, legally speaking, they completely overlooked their potential liability for future discrimination claims.

Here's why. A supervisor's derogatory comments about an employee's gender, race or religion may not amount to a harassment claim. But they are a smoking gun in a later discrimination claim.

The Discrimination Blind Spot

Discrimination claims are all about the supervisor's frame of mind when he or she made a decision about an employee promotion, compensation or firing. But since we can't read someone's mind, the only thing we have to go on is their comments and behavior.

If a supervisor makes objectifying comments about a woman's body and then later denies her a promotion, those comments may later be used to show his decision was biased.

The Nike story offers a great illustration of this principle. A manager who views women primarily in terms of condom consumption is probably not also thinking of them as a potential vice president candidate. Nevertheless, it is unsurprising to me that Nike's human resources department seemingly failed to identify the problem as discrimination when employees complained.

And that's because, in all likelihood, the discrimination had not yet happened. When the woman complained, it probably wasn't yet about a lost promotion, unfair compensation or a termination. It was "just" a comment.

Of course, to the employee, it was never just a comment. She would have been keenly aware that her career was in her supervisor's hands. And that he could no longer be trusted.

This is not really a rare occurrence for women in the US. In representative samples, around 25 percent to 40 percent of women report having experienced unwanted sexually based behaviors at work, and 60 percent said they encountered hostile behaviors or comments based on their gender.

It's as though the employee can see the gun and anticipates the bullet to come. But all human resources sees is a weak harassment complaint unworthy of intervention.

A Better Way

The #MeToo movement has generated discussion around "zero tolerance" harassment policies, containing perhaps the implied threat that even minor transgressions of the policy will be met with strong punishment.

But because harassment policies already cover the waterfront, they don't really provide meaningful behavioral guidance. A Pew Research study published in March found that half of all adults surveyed thought that #MeToo made it harder for "men to know how to interact with women in the workplace."

I actually think a more sustainable approach—which actually better aligns with a company's true legal risks—would be to beef up anti-discrimination policies.

These policies would explain that supervisors are placed in a special position of trust regarding their subordinates' careers and that supervisors act as the company's proxy in carrying out the employer's duty to provide equal employment opportunities.

When a supervisor engages in low-level harassing behaviors or makes derogatory comments based on a employee's gender, race or religion, it is a breach of that trust.

And it is the company's duty to make it right.

EVALUATING THE AUTHOR'S ARGUMENTS:

In this viewpoint, Elizabeth C. Tippett suggests that the legal definition of harassment may not do enough to protect employees. She suggests focusing on discrimination instead. Do you think this would help reduce harassment at work? How else could companies handle the problem?

Lose Famous People and You Also Lose Great Art

> *"Why not include the other arts in the clean-up and stop revering the paintings of Picasso, Gauguin or Degas?"*

Margaret Leclere

In the following viewpoint, Margaret Leclere argues that we should not dismiss and ignore an artist's past work because the artist has been revealed as an unsavory person. The Auteur Theory refers to a theory in filmmaking where the director is viewed as the "author," or major creative force, in a movie. These directors were seen as geniuses and given great power. However, some of them have also been accused of crimes. The author suggests that the film industry's system that empowered male artists to exploit and abuse women should be ended. Margaret Leclere is a Senior Lecturer in Screenwriting in the English & Creative Writing Department at Staffordshire University.

AS YOU READ, CONSIDER THE FOLLOWING QUESTIONS:

1. What is the Auteur Theory and how has it affected filmmaking?
2. How could having great power as a director allow someone to harass or abuse those working with him?
3. What comparison does the author draw between film directors and painters or writers?

Behavior that once went unpunished and may even have been encouraged, like that of Bill Cosby, is no longer tolerated. Should we mourn the lost careers and legacies of these offenders?

The Auteur Theory, which has held the film industry and film criticism in its grip since the 1950s, has recently come under attack from film critics – until now its greatest champions. The problem they face is that many of the directors deified as auteurs have been caught up in the #MeToo movement's sweep of the film industry.

Film critic Ryan Gilbey writes of the atrocities wrought by the Auteur Theory and asks what happens when a God-like director turns out to be a liability. He ends his piece with the line:

> *It is difficult to see how the unquestioning reverence of directors can continue in this new climate of hyperawareness, where the constant drip-feed of discrediting stories proves once and for all that time's up.*

Time may be up, but #MeToo is not a critically sound basis for renouncing the Auteur Theory. Its faults need greater scrutiny. The foundation stone for the theory can be found in one paragraph from a thoughtful 1948 essay by the film-maker Alexandre Astruc, in which he sought to identify a new age of cinema: the age of the camera-stylo (camera-pen):

Direction is no longer a means of illustrating or presenting a scene, but a true act of writing. The film-maker/author writes with his camera as a writer writes with his pen.

Astruc considered the future of cinema to be dependent upon there being a single creator (a scriptwriter who directs his own scripts —like Woody Allen). After all, as he says: "Could one imagine a Faulkner novel written by someone other than Faulkner?" His aim was to push cinema towards being taken seriously as an art form, rather than remaining "a fairground attraction". Yet it was the line: "the film maker/author writes with his camera as a writer writes with his pen" that launched the Auteur Thoery and the cult of the director.

Astruc's argument was twisted but his aim was achieved: cinema could now be considered an art form, with a single creative mind in control—the director. This led eventually to the use of the notorious possessory credit which states that the film is "by" the director, regardless of who wrote the screenplay. This happens even when the screenplay is an original idea, written before a director is attached to the project.

The Auteur Tyranny

The Auteur Theory became a tyranny, McCarthyite in its single-mindedness. Horribly, lists of auteur directors were drawn up, notably by American film critic Andrew Sarris. Those whose names were not on the list had been judged by critical opinion to be lesser directors. John Huston, for example, never made the list. His extraordinary number of great films failed to display the kind of mono-style that marked out the true auteur, aiming instead for a style appropriate to the literary source.

Yet the fact remains that over the decades it held sway, the focus on the director meant that many artists working in film flourished and produced masterpieces. Among the discredited auteurs cited by Gilbey are Woody Allen and Roman Polanski, whose names would feature in most critics' lists of the greatest geniuses of cinema—along with Chaplin, Hitchcock, Kubrick and Welles. It is through their innovations that film achieved its modern ability to rival the novel in depth and subtlety.

Art and Ethics

But if cinema is an art form, then why treat it differently from the other arts? Conversely, why not include the other arts in the clean-up and stop revering the paintings of Picasso, Gauguin or Degas? Or stop reading the works of Lewis Carroll or Vladimir Nabokov, just in case? Let us not look at anything made by anybody who is, in Margaret Attwood's phrase, "guilty by allegation" (like Woody Allen).

Reviewing Allen's latest film *Wonder Wheel* in *The Times*, Kevin Maher found it necessary to ditch discussion of the film's director altogether, only mentioning Allen in the final sentence:

> *The film was written and directed by Woody Allen. In 1993 he was accused of molesting his adopted daughter … He denied the accusations and was never prosecuted. Should you go and see it? Over to you.*

And what of Roman Polanski, who actually admitted a statutory rape charge in 1977? If Allen's films are suspect, Polanski's must be even more so. It does not for one moment excuse his crime to insist that his work in cinema has taught and inspired generations of film makers, with some of his films even claimed by young feminists. Must we now avert our eyes?

Where Will This End?

Charlie Chaplin, possibly the greatest auteur the world has known, made all his films before the Auteur Theory existed. Chaplin wrote, directed, starred in and composed the music for his movies. His stature as an artist is arguably on a level with Picasso. Of Picasso, the novelist Caroline Blackwood—speaking from personal experience—said: "He was an old letch, genius or no." Perhaps something similar could be said of Chaplin.

The artistic drive and the sex drive have always been closely linked. The adoration of the human form, the fascination with the object of desire, driving the creation of works of art, or simply driving the artist. Tracey Emin's work is as sexually driven as Hitchcock's, or as her hero, Egon Schiele's. To deny this, to attempt to outlaw it, is an act of cultural suicide.

There is no doubt that a line—first drawn by the early feminists—has been underscored by #MeToo. The attitudes that once enabled male artists to exploit and abuse women with impunity must be cast into the past. But leave the work alone, with its cultural life living on beyond its creators. And as far as cinema is concerned, simply calling time on the already waning Auteur Theory does not accomplish anything at all. It's perhaps time for a new theory.

EVALUATING THE AUTHOR'S ARGUMENTS:

In this viewpoint, Margaret Leclere suggests that we need a new way of treating great artists. The new method should allow them to create great art but not allow them to exploit and abuse others. Does she explain what this method should be? Can you think of possible options?

You Can't Separate the Artist from the Art

"Art makers and their audiences become emotionally attached to artists and composers as individuals."

Irina Aristarkhova

In the following viewpoint, Irina Aristarkhova discusses visual artists who have been accused of sexual harassment. Two famous men had art exhibits canceled after allegations were made against them. The author notes that some people believe artwork is separate from the morality of the artists. Other people believe the artists and their work are intertwined. No matter how much of a genius an artist is, they should not be allowed to harm other people, this author feels. Irina Aristarkhova is associate professor of women's studies and visual art at Pennsylvania State University.

AS YOU READ, CONSIDER THE FOLLOWING QUESTIONS:

1. When did people start to see sexual harassment as evil?
2. How did the #MeToo movement affect the visual art world, according to the author?
3. How did sexual harassment affect the victims, according to those mentioned in the viewpoint?

Cancelled exhibitions at the National Gallery of Art and other museums and galleries have brought to light the relationship between art and its treatment of women, among other controversial issues.

This May, the National Gallery of Art in Washington, DC, was to showcase the work of two famous artists: one of painter Chuck Close and another of photographer Thomas Roma. Both exhibitions, however were cancelled due to allegations of sexual harassment.

The public debate sparked by the cancellations has centered around the question, is it possible to separate the value of art from the personal conduct of the artist?

As a scholar of aesthetics and gender studies, I believe, in the wake of #MeToo this is a good time to revisit the argument of Russian poet Alexander Pushkin about the incompatibility of genius and evil.

Genius and Evil

In his short play from 1830, *Mozart and Salieri*, Pushkin fictionalizes an encounter between the composer Antonio Salieri and his younger friend, Wolfgang Amadeus Mozart, in Vienna, Austria. Based on existing rumors at the time, Pushkin presents Salieri as envious of Mozart's genius to the point of poisoning him at the meeting.

Pushkin's claim in this play was that the human value of good defines genius, and hence committing a crime disqualifies one from being a genius. Based on this presentation of Salieri as evil, his reputation as a composer was tarnished.

After new research suggested that Mozart died from natural causes, most probably a strep infection, views on Salieri's music also changed. With this new information, Pushkin's argument was revisited, and Salieri's reputation in the music community started to improve, demonstrated by recorded albums and staging of his operas.

This goes to show how art makers and their audiences become emotionally attached to artists and composers as individuals, and not just to their music or painting. Pushkin himself identified strongly with Mozart.

And the change in attitudes to Salieri also supports Pushkin's original argument that how genius is understood is strongly correlated with human values, where good and genius reinforce each other.

The Debate

In the current debate in the art world over this issue, several experts have said that the value of art should not be associated with the personal conduct of its maker. For example, Tom Eccles, executive director of the Center for Curatorial Studies at Bard College, suggested that "we can't not show artists because we don't agree with them morally; we'd have fairly bare walls." An example would be be that of the famous painter Caravaggio, who was accused of murder and whose works continue to be on display.

However, James Rondeau, the president and director of the Art Institute of Chicago, disagreed that museums could present their decisions about the value of the artwork as totally separate from today's ethics. Rondeau said:

> *"The typical 'we don't judge, we don't endorse, we just put it up for people to experience and decide' falls very flat in this political and cultural moment."*

The #MeToo Ethical Challenge

This public debate has gained significant traction in the art world because the #MeToo movement has redefined sexual harassment as evil. Started by Tarana Burke, an African-American civil rights activist in 2006 and spread by Alyssa Milano, an American actress and activist, as a Twitter campaign in 2017, the #MeToo movement has become a social media-driven collective voice. It has presented sexual harassment and sexual violence as harm serious enough to warrant recognition and social change.

Consequently, a number of artists have come out with their experience of sexual harassment. Five women came forward accusing Thomas Roma, a photographer and professor, of sexual misconduct. In the case of Chuck Close, artists Langdon Graves, Delia Brown and Julia Fox described in interviews and on social media platforms the anguish and self-doubt his actions had caused them as individuals and also as artists.

Delia Brown, for example, described how Chuck Close told her at a dinner that he was a fan of her work and asked her to pose for a portrait at his studio. She said she was "over the moon" and excited "because having your portrait done as an artist by Chuck Close is tantamount to being canonized."

However, she was shocked when he asked her to model topless, not a practice that he pursued with other famous artists. Brown refused. Explaining her anguish, she felt he saw her only as a body rather than an important artist and felt manipulated. She said "a sense of distrust and disgust" has stayed with her. Other artists made similar allegations of having been invited to Close's studio to pose for him and being shocked by his behavior.

Chuck Close chose to downplay the harm done to them as persons and artists by dismissing their words. He said the "last time I looked, discomfort was not a major offense."

Genius Redefined

The point this reinforces is that if sexual harassment is wrong then the value of artwork being exhibited in a public museum is questionable.

Scholar Roxane Gay, the best-selling author of the essay collection "Bad Feminist," sums up why it is so evil, when she explains the cost to women. She says:

> *"I remember how many women's careers were ruined; I think of those who gave up their dreams because some 'genius' decided indulging his thirst for power and control mattered more than her ambition and dignity. I remember all the silence, decades and decades of enforced silence, intimidation, and manipulation, that enabled bad men to flourish. When I do that, it's quite easy for me to think nothing of the supposedly great art of bad men."*

This debate has also shown how the definitions of evil in Pushkin's "genius and evil" argument are also subjective and depend on human values at a particular time. #MeToo has changed the public view on sexual harassment. Indeed, the public debate surrounding the decision by the National Gallery of Art to cancel two exhibitions has been as much about the value of human beings as it has been about the value of art.

EVALUATING THE AUTHOR'S ARGUMENTS:

In this viewpoint, the author suggests that an artist's personal life cannot be separated from their art. Compare this to the previous viewpoint. Who makes a stronger case? Why? Does it matter if the artist is living or deceased?

Chapter 3

How Should We Handle Accusations Against Public Figures?

Is the shame brought about by the court of public opinion sufficiently effective? Is it fair?

The Media Should Stop Supporting Rape Culture

Lindsey Blumell

"[B]ecause a powerful accuser is more or less guaranteed to be listened to, this sort of coverage can actually end up advancing myths about rape and sexual misconduct."

In the following viewpoint, Lindsey Blumell argues that, while some men finally are losing jobs over sexual harrassment accusations, the media tends to pay more attention to the words of the famous accused men than to their accusers. This gives the men the opportunity to frame the discussion in their favor. In addition, journalists who report on sexual harassment can reinforce the myths about it. They may quote people who blame the victim or falsely state that many women lie about being assaulted. By quoting people who reinforce rape culture, the media helps perpetuate rape culture. Lindsey Blumell is a journalism lecturer at City University London.

AS YOU READ, CONSIDER THE FOLLOWING QUESTIONS:
1. Whose claims get more coverage, those accused of sexual harassment or their victims?
2. How do journalists who attempt to report stories objectively actually support myths?
3. How does the media sometimes support victim blaming when reporting on criminal accusations?

When Fox News host Bill O'Reilly was finally fired after years of sexual harassment claims, it seemed like a welcome break from the norm: an exceptionally powerful man accused of sexual misconduct was for once not protected at all costs. While various harassment claims against Donald Trump failed to stop him in his path to the White House, O'Reilly, it seems, was not as invulnerable as he thought.

Yet while these two men faced very different outcomes, their cases have a lot in common. Crucially, the coverage of and public reaction to these incidents in fact reinforced some of the core elements of rape culture—a pervasive set of ideas and beliefs that normalise and even condone sexual misconduct in general, ultimately protecting perpetrators at the expense of victims.

But wait. Wasn't O'Reilly brought down by a *New York Times* investigation? Wasn't it the *Washington Post* who obtained the infamous tape of Trump caught bragging about sexually assaulting women with impunity? Yes It's time to interrogate the role the media plays in protecting high-profile men accused of sexual misconduct, and in perpetuating the insidious myths they benefit from.

All branches of the media, particularly television news, rely heavily on sources to provide insight and commentary on any story—and from a producer or editor's point of view, the more important the source, the better. The problem is that the most powerful sources are the best placed to shape the coverage with their words, no matter how outlandish or absurd. The upshot is that the intense coverage of these cases gives the accused themselves far more attention than their accusers.

Trump, for instance, responded to the scandal over the *Access Hollywood* tape by calling an extraordinary press conference hours

What message do we send when the President of the United States of America has been accused of sexual misconduct by more than 15 women and gone completely unchecked?

before his second debate with Hillary Clinton, at which he was flanked by women who'd levelled sexual misconduct allegations at Bill Clinton—a man not even running for office. He then brought these women with him to the debate and pointed them out in the audience.

Trump's publicity stunt clearly wasn't an effort to win justice for Bill Clinton's accusers. It was designed first to smear Hillary Clinton with guilt by association, and to tell voters that whatever accusations were levelled against Trump were far from unique and therefore somehow tolerable, while still of course denying they were credible at all.

Of course, the accuseds' reactions to the allegations directed at them need to be included in news coverage. But Trump's own words were given dramatically more exposure than those of his accusers, whose own stories and points of view simply did not generate anything like the same coverage.

This is compounded by a well-intentioned tradition of attempting to report stories "objectively" by presenting the point of view of both sides—but because a powerful accuser is more or less guaranteed

FAST FACT

Rape culture refers to the ways that society normalizes male sexual violence and blames the victims of sexual assaults.

to be listened to, this sort of coverage can actually end up advancing myths about rape and sexual misconduct.

However incorrect these myths are, they are both enduring and shockingly widespread. The ones that most often surface in news coverage are that victims are to blame, that sexual misbehaviour just isn't as important as other issues, and that women who come forward are relatively likely to have fabricated their stories—and they must therefore be treated sceptically.

Taking Control

O'Reilly has publicly peddled the unsubstantiated statement that women falsely accuse powerful men of sexual assault in order to ruin their careers and for personal profit. If a list were made of all the famous, wealthy, powerful men in Western societies, the proportion who have been accused of sexual misconduct and then formally sanctioned for it would be conspicuously small.

When the accusations against him began to mount, the far less articulate Trump also sought to discredit the integrity of his accusers a different way: "Look at her, I don't think so…" And once again, his words rather than his accusers' dominated the ensuing coverage.

Victim-blaming is more and more widely recognised as wrong, but it's still both very common and disturbingly powerful. In the aftermath of the *Access Hollywood* tape debacle, many Trump surrogates, including Scottie Nell Hughes, tried to dismiss the women coming forward on the pretext that it was suspicious that they didn't immediately report what had happened to them. Sarah Palin invoked the same idea during the O'Reilly debacle.

These ideas not only shift the responsibility for dealing with sexual assault onto victims, but also ignore evidence the majority of women who experience workplace sexual misconduct never report it. These myths are all the more powerful when propagated by female sources such as Hughes and Palin: if the accusers were credible, the logic goes, surely other women wouldn't dismiss them?

As was made clear in the home stretch of the US election, powerful men accused of sexual misconduct can even turn the media attention they get to their advantage. When asked about sexual assault and the *Access Hollywood* tape, Trump and his surrogates were able to plead with the media and public to refocus the campaign on "important" issues—and now he's president, as far as the media is concerned, it's almost as if the astonishing claims against him had never been made.

Coverage of the extremely serious claims against Trump quickly faded after the *Access Hollywood* story had played out, and Trump is now president. But the O'Reilly case is perhaps cause for encouragement. Women have been accusing him of misbehaviour for years with little or no effect on his career—but now it appears even as powerful a figure as him is no longer guaranteed effective impunity.

Whatever the reason for this change, it is to be welcomed. In the interests of the victims of sexual misconduct everywhere, hopefully the media will keep up the pressure.

EVALUATING THE AUTHOR'S ARGUMENTS:

In this viewpoint, Lindsey Blumell argues that famous men are still often protected when accused of sexual harassment and that the media has a role in this due to the way stories are reported. Can the media practice objective reporting (telling both sides of the story) without letting powerful men have the loudest and final say? What changes should be made in the way stories are reported, if any?

Viewpoint

2

Believe Innocent Until Proven Guilty

Roger E. Olson

"Many innocent people's lives have been destroyed by rushes to judgment based solely on their being accused of sex crimes."

In the following viewpoint, Roger E. Olson questions whether our society really believes people are innocent until proven guilty. He suggests that the media and the public often assume people are guilty as soon as they're accused. Even when people are found innocent, the public exposure and false accusations can haunt them for life. The author argues that people accused of sex crimes should especially have their names protected until and unless they are found guilty. Otherwise they might unfairly suffer for crimes they did not commit. Roger E. Olson is a Professor of Theology at Baylor University, Texas.

AS YOU READ, CONSIDER THE FOLLOWING QUESTIONS:

1. What two ways can people be found guilty by a court of law?
2. How can the language used to describe accused people support the idea that they are guilty?
3. How can businesses protect other employees and customers when an employee is accused of rape, according to the author?

"Innocent until Proven Guilty? Or Guilty until Proven Innocent?" by Roger E. Olson, Foy Valentine Professor of Theology and Christian Ethics, Baylor University, Roger E. Olson, February 25, 2017. Reprinted by permission.

Has mob justice, now delivered through social media and the 24-hour news cycle, become preferable to the US justice system?

All my life I've heard the mantra "innocent until proven guilty" as one expression of our American justice system. It means, of course, "until proven guilty beyond a reasonable doubt in a court of law by a jury of one's peers." And, I learned, as I grew older, there are exceptions. A defendant can, for example, plead guilty or he can request his case to be heard and decided by a judge instead of a jury.

However, underlying all that, and given those few exceptions, basic to our American system of justice is the well-known principle that a person accused of committing a crime should be considered innocent until she is found guilty beyond a reasonable doubt.

As an ethicist, however, I question whether we, as a society, really abide by that principle. I think we should work harder at it.

Too often persons accused of crimes are tried and, for all practical purposes, declared guilty long before any trial is held (or they confess to the crimes). How does this happen? In a recent case, reported in the newspaper, a man was accused of and charged with a sexual misdemeanor; his name and picture were printed and some people

FAST FACT

According to the Rape,
Abuse & Incest National
Network (RAINN), out
of every 1000 rapes, an
estimated 310 are reported
to police. Of those, only six
rapists are incarcerated.

who knew him were quoted as assuming his guilt. This is not an isolated incident; it happens all too often.

A few years ago I was privileged to serve in a "jury pool." During the "voir dire," during which the prosecutor and the defense attorney questioned us to discover our fitness to serve on this particular jury, several potential jurors expressed the opinion that the defendant, an African-American man sitting in the same room, "must have done something or he wouldn't be here." I suspect that opinion is very common.

Memories are too short. In 2006 three Duke University lacrosse players were falsely accused of and charged with rape; they were villainized in the media. Some television "crime journalists" tried them and found them guilty long before the evidence was in and the case dropped. The charges against them were dismissed and a prosecutor was disbarred for prosecutorial misconduct. And yet, their lives were forever altered by the false accusation and public exposure.

We should have re-learned a lesson from that and numerous other examples of cases in which people accused and charged with crimes turned out to be truly innocent. The lesson is that "innocent until proven guilty" is more than an empty mantra; it is a principle to be followed by everyone—including the media and employers.

If I had my way (which I sadly don't expect), the identities of persons accused especially of sex crimes would not be revealed until they either confess or are found guilty beyond a reasonable doubt by a judge (as they choose) or jury of their peers—all of who know what "innocent until proven guilty" means.

I support caution in such cases. No doubt employers and others should know about the accusation and charge and either suspend the accused with pay or quarantine him from contact with potential victims.

Very often, however, public language about such accused persons, points to a presumption of their guilt. They are often referred to as "perpetrators" long before any due process has been conducted and concluded.

Speaking up on behalf of persons accused of sex crimes is not comfortable; I have no doubt that some readers will think I am "soft on crime." That is not the case; I am simply calling for us all, including especially the media, to take more seriously the principle "innocent until proven guilty." Many innocent people's lives have been destroyed by rushes to judgment based solely on their being accused of (especially but not only) sex crimes. Their families have also been severely affected by their father's, brother's or son's picture being published in what amounts to a modern equivalent of the antiquated "perp walk."

Yes, the public has "a right to know," but I would argue that right should not override an accused person's right to be considered truly innocent until proven guilty. And that does not seem possible—given our society's tendency to believe the worst about the accused—when their pictures and identities are published for all to see. So the only solution is to protect the accused's privacy until she either confesses or is found guilty "beyond a reasonable doubt" in court.

EVALUATING THE AUTHOR'S ARGUMENTS:

In this viewpoint, Roger E. Olson suggests that people who have been accused of sex crimes have a right to privacy. What are the benefits and pitfalls of protecting versus publicizing the names of people accused of crimes? Should people only suffer for their crimes if they have been found guilty in a court of law? Or should people accused of crimes be subjected to other forms of punishment, such as public shaming or losing their job, even if they are not convicted?

Viewpoint 3

We May Never Know Innocence or Guilt

Cathy Young

"Even in a good cause, you have to try to check the facts."

In the following excerpted viewpoint, Cathy Young reviews coverage of an alleged rape at Columbia University in which the accused and accuser's versions of the story differ widely. The accused was not tried by the legal system, but the university investigated and dismissed the allegations. Still, he suffered because of the accusations. Meanwhile, the accuser feels justice has not been done. The author notes that it is impossible to know the truth of the matter, but the accused, despite being exonerated by the system, has still been treated as guilty in some ways. Cathy Young is a contributing editor for *Reason* magazine and a weekly columnist for *Newsday*.

AS YOU READ, CONSIDER THE FOLLOWING QUESTIONS:

1. What complaints did the accused and the accuser each have about the way the university handled the case?
2. How did the accused suffer once his name was made public?
3. What complaints did the accused and his family have about the media coverage of this case?

Proving innocence or guilt is not always a simple endeavor. And sometimes, neither is agreeing on what actually happened.

The Columbia University senior vividly remembers the day, in April 2013, when he received a phone call while working in the school's digital architecture lab. It was the campus Office of Gender-Based and Sexual Misconduct, asking him to come in to talk. At the time, he says, he was not particularly alarmed: "I thought initially that maybe they called me in as a witness."

Instead, Paul Nungesser, a full-scholarship student from Germany, found himself at the center of a sexual-assault case that would eventually receive national media coverage and attract the attention of politicians and feminist leaders. Nungesser's accuser, Emma Sulkowicz—famous for carrying her mattress on campus as a symbol of her burden as a victim and a protest against Columbia's failure to expel the man she calls her rapist—has become the face of the college rape survivors' movement

[…]

The story Sulkowicz has told, in numerous media appearances and interviews, is nothing short of harrowing. On Aug. 27, 2012, she has said, a sexual encounter that began as consensual suddenly turned terrifyingly violent: Her partner, a man whom she consid-ered a close friend and with whom she had sex on two prior occa-sions, began choking and hitting her and then penetrated her anally while she struggled and screamed in pain. By Sulkowicz's account, she finally decided to file a complaint within the university system several months later when she heard stories of other sexual assaults by the same man—only to see him exonerated after a shoddy inves-tigation and a hearing at which she was subjected to clueless and insensitive questions. What's more, charges brought against the man by two other women also ended up being dismissed.

[...]

In the coverage of Sulkowicz and her battle for redress, her alleged assailant remained, until recently, a shadowy faceless villain. While Nungesser's name was first made public in May 2014 after Sulkowicz filed a police report, he did his best to keep a low profile until last December, when he spoke to *The New York Times* for a story that focused on his and his accusers' conflicting perceptions of the case and on Nungesser's pariah status at Columbia. Now, Nungesser has agreed to speak to *The Daily Beast* and tell his version of the events. This story, partly backed by materials made public here for the first time and corroborated by a former Columbia graduate student who played a secondary role in the disciplinary process, is dramatically at odds with the prevailing media narrative. On one point, however, Nungesser and his supporters agree with the pro-Sulkowicz camp: A grave injustice has been done.

Seated in the same room where he once received that fateful call, now empty on a non-class day, Nungesser looks back on his rela-tionship with Sulkowicz. They got to know each other in their fresh-man year, he says, mainly as fellow leaders in the Columbia Outdoor Orientation Program (COÖP), a freshman pre-orientation experi-ence with a focus on outdoor activities. Sulkowicz also rushed Alpha Delta Phi (ADP), a coed fraternity with a literary and intellectual bent, which Nungesser joined a few months later. By the end of his first year in college in spring 2012, says Nungesser, "we were begin-ning to develop a very close friendship; it was an intimate friendship where we would hug each other and so on, but always platonic." That platonic friendship included several sleepovers in Sulkowicz's room—one of which, he says, eventually turned into a make-out session and ended in sex.

"The next morning, we had a talk about it and we both felt that it was not really a good idea," says Nungesser, explaining that they didn't want to risk their friendship. Four or five weeks later, he says, there was another sleepover that led to another sexual encounter, another talk, and another decision to move on—soon after which the two parted ways for the summer break.

After a summer of affectionate and often intimate Facebook chats (screenshots of which Nungesser, who has since deactivated all of his social-media accounts, provided to *The Daily Beast*), Nungesser and Sulkowicz returned to Columbia in late August and saw each other at an end-of-summer party for COÖP leaders. As the party was wrapping up, they started talking in the courtyard, then began to hug and kiss and ended up going back to Sulkowicz's dorm room—at her invitation, according to Nungesser. He says he had consumed two mixed drinks and was "buzzed, but not intoxicated or anything." (Sulkowicz has previously described him as "drunk" during the incident.)

While Sulkowicz has always said that they started out having consensual sex, her account diverges drastically from Nungesser's at this point. According to Sulkowicz, he suddenly and brutally assaulted her, then picked up his clothes and left without a word, leaving her stunned and shattered on the bed. According to Nungesser, they briefly engaged in anal intercourse by mutual agreement, then went on to engage in other sexual activity and fell asleep. He says that he woke up early in the morning and went back to his own room while Sulkowicz was still sleeping.

Sulkowicz has said in interviews that she was too embarrassed and ashamed to talk to anyone about the rape, let alone report it; an account of her mattress protest by *New York Times* art critic Roberta Smith says that she "suffered in silence" in the aftermath of the assault. Yet Nungesser says that for weeks after that night, he and Sulkowicz maintained a cordial relationship, and says she seemingly never indicated that anything was amiss.

[...]

On Oct. 3, Sulkowicz's birthday, Nungesser sent her an effusive greeting; she responded the next morning with, "I love you Paul.

Where are you?!?!?!?!" Nungesser claims that these exchanges represent only a small portion of their friendly communications, which also included numerous text messages. But he also says that during those weeks, they were starting to drift apart; they saw each other at meetings and parties, but plans for one-on-one get-togethers always seemed to end in "missed connections." Nungesser says that he assumed it was simply a matter of hanging out with a new crowd and, in Sulkowicz's case, being in a new relationship. He says that "it was very amiable; nothing was changed or different or weird or anything in her behavior." (To be sure, many rape victims' advocates would argue that women traumatized by sexual violence, especially by someone they trusted and cared about, may deal with trauma in ways that don't make sense to an observer.)

[...]

On April 18, when Nungesser came to the Office of Gender-Based and Sexual Misconduct, he was informed that Sulkowicz had filed a complaint accusing him of sexual assault. He was given no specific details—not until a meeting with the school's Title IX investigator nearly two weeks later.

"My first reaction was, 'It has to be a misunderstanding,'" says Nungesser. "Maybe she meant a different guy, or something completely strange happened."

Even before the investigation began, the charge had immediate consequences. Nungesser was placed on restricted access to university buildings other than his own dorm; these "interim measures" made it extremely difficult to continue in his campus job as an audiovisual technician (especially since he was not allowed to explain why he was under these restrictions) and to attend the counseling sessions he had started. Meanwhile, it became obvious that despite confidentiality rules, news of the accusation was spreading: Within a few days, Nungesser says he was being conspicuously shunned by many fellow students.

[...]

On May 3, one day before the end of classes, Nungesser was given notice of two new complaints. One was from a former girlfriend who was alleging that he had emotionally and sexually abused her for the duration of that relationship. The other one was from a fellow resident at ADP, a senior who claimed that over a year earlier, in April 2012, he had followed her upstairs during a house party after offering to help her get more beer to restock the bar, then grabbed her and tried to kiss her. Due to the second complaint, the Office of Gender-Based and Sexual Misconduct sent Nungesser an email instructing him to vacate his room at ADP the next day "to ensure the safety of all the parties involved in this matter" and move to another dorm for the brief remainder of the school year.

As Nungesser headed back to Germany for the summer break, matters looked grim for his future at Columbia, with three different women now accusing him of sexual assault. Yet by the end of the year, he had been cleared by all charges. To Nungesser and his parents, who helped hire a criminal attorney for him and stood by his side throughout the process, this outcome is a victory for justice.

Of course, to Sulkowicz's supporters, the case is a travesty of malignant distrust toward women who accuse men of sexual violence, all the more blatant when it's multiple women accusing the same man.

Last April, a press release from the office of Sen. Gillibrand on the problem of campus sexual assault quoted Sulkowicz as saying, "My rapist—a serial rapist—still remains on campus, even though three of the women he assaulted reported him."

Actually, only one of the charges against Nungesser was a clear allegation of rape. What's more, there are indications that the accusations may not have been completely independent of each other.

[...]

In December 2013, shortly before flying to Germany for the winter break, Nungesser says he received an email from *The New York Post* giving him a few hours to respond for a story about his case (he did not) and then had to dodge *Post* photographers outside his building. The *Post* story, which described him as an entitled campus jock who had gotten away with multiple sexual assaults "because the school dropped the ball on investigating him," ran on Dec. 11. In spring, while Nungesser was in Prague, Sulkowicz went public, appearing at a press conference with Sen. Gillibrand and then on the front page of *The New York Times*.

[...]

Nungesser's anonymity was increasingly precarious: In early May, lists of campus "rapists" and "sexual-assault violators" began to show up in bathrooms in several Columbia dorms, with his name topping the list as a "serial rapist." Then, on May 14, Sulkowicz filed a police report. In her comments to *The Columbia Spectator*, she said: "Maybe his name should be in the public record." And indeed, *The Columbia Spectator* story included Nungesser's name.

Sulkowicz ultimately elected not to pursue criminal charges (she has been quoted as saying that it would be "too draining"). According to Nungesser's criminal defense attorney, Daniel Parker, Nungesser voluntarily met and spoke with two Manhattan assistant district attorneys in August and was later informed that no charges would be brought against him. Yet, as Nungesser returned to the Columbia campus, the notoriety of his case exploded with Sulkowicz's mattress protest.

Sulkowicz's act, which is also her senior project for her visual arts degree, has been praised as both protest and art. To Nungesser, however, it is something else altogether: harassment. "It's explicitly designed to bully me into leaving the school—she has said so repeatedly," he says, referring to Sulkowicz's statement that she will carry the mattress until either Nungesser leaves Columbia or they both graduate. "That is not art. If she was doing this for artistic self-expression, or exploration of her identity—all these are valid motives. Scaring another student into leaving university is not a valid motive."

Nungesser also says he has been the target of social-media threats. A Tumblr post that began to circulate last September said, "The name of Emma Sulkowicz's rapist is Jean-Paul Nungesser. Don't let him have any feeling of anonymity or security. Rapists don't get the luxury of feeling comfortable." Around the same time, Nungesser says that he and his parents spotted an eventually removed a Facebook post that had a far more ominous tone, stating, "I'm only pissed that I'm not in NY to CUT HIS THROAT MYSELF!"

[…]

"What really struck us as outrageously unfair," says Nungesser's father, Andreas Probosch, a schoolteacher who speaks near-perfect English, "was the university's non-reaction to Emma Sulkowicz's public campaign. After investigating the allegations against Paul for seven months they found them not credible, but when Ms. Sulkowicz went to the press and claimed Columbia had swept everything under the rug, why didn't they stand by his side and say, 'We do have a process and we followed that process and we stand by the acquittal'? Instead they declined to comment and just threw him under the bus."

Both Probosch and Nungesser express bafflement at the practice of letting colleges handle allegations of violent rape. But if such a process must exist, says Probosch, "doesn't [it] only make sense if people accept its outcome?" In this case, he says, "Paul went through this whole process with endless hours of hearings and interviews and cooperated in every way possible. And yet if you Google him, in half of the articles you'll find, he is still labeled a serial rapist."

For Nungesser's mother, Karin, the situation is laden with additional irony as a self-described committed feminist. Paul Nungesser's comment to *The New York Times*, "My mother raised me as a feminist," caused predictable controversy; but his mother, at least, agrees. She points out that she and her husband took an equal role in parenting and that gender issues, which were part of her journalistic work, were often discussed in their home when her son was growing up: "I think we did not just tell him that men and women are created equal, but we lived it."

Karin Nungesser fully understands the desire to support someone who comes forward with an accusation of rape: "This is a good cause—but even in a good cause, you have to try to check the facts." What she views as the failure to check the facts in this case appalls her not only as a feminist but as a journalist. "We can't understand to this day why the major media never asked Paul about his side," she says. "Going back to our own history, the media in western Germany were built upon the model of *The New York Times*. It was the idea of good journalism, of good fact-checking, of not doing propaganda."

It is likely that some facts in this case will never be known. Nungesser's feminist upbringing does not make him incapable of sexual assault, and his former girlfriend's reported psychological problems prior to their relationship do not mean that he did not abuse her. The reported interaction between Nungesser's alleged victims does not necessarily prove that they unduly influenced each other's stories.

Yet this case is far from as clear-cut as much of the media coverage has made it out to be. And if Nungesser is not a sexual predator, he could be seen as a true victim: a man who has been treated as guilty even after he has proved his innocence.

EVALUATING THE AUTHOR'S ARGUMENTS:

In this viewpoint, Cathy Young notes that someone who has been accused of sexual assault can suffer even if they are found innocent. Should the media refuse to name those accused of crimes until after they are found guilty? Do victims have the right to publicly shame their attackers if the system does not punish those people?

Viewpoint

4

Don't Minimize the Problem

Nesrine Malik

"Something deep in their DNA is telling them that their status is unearned."

In the following viewpoint, Nesrine Malik discusses backlash against the #MeToo movement. She claims that men are hysterically complaining that the movement has gone too far. Some of those men claim that any slight attention to women might now be called sexual harassment. Thus, men don't know how to behave and are afraid of repercussions. The author argues that these complaints are simply people in power trying to hold onto their power. They minimize and dismiss the problem of sexual harassment so they don't have to change their own behavior. Nesrine Malik is a columnist for the *Guardian*.

AS YOU READ, CONSIDER THE FOLLOWING QUESTIONS:
1. How does the patriarchy survive, according to the author?
2. How are complaints about the #MeToo movement designed to minimize the problem of sexual harassment?
3. Why do men and some women want to downplay the problem of sexual harassment,?

The reaction of many powerful men to the #MeToo movement has revealed that the deep-rooted system of patriarchy will not be easy to undo.

I know it feels like years, but we are only just over three weeks into the post-Weinstein "#MeToo" ramifications on media and politics. There is a cultural shift under way. Those in power, who hitherto were immune, are beginning to understand that there are consequences. But even though some big names have been challenged, it is only the beginning of a correction. Barely even that. It is the beginning of a hope of a correction.

Yet even this is too much for many. Almost every day now, there is a man on the radio or the television telling us that things have gone too far. Almost every day, there is a man's sneering, hovering head sitting on top of a few hundred words of what is really no less than the sort of existential hysteria of an animal whose cosy ecosystem has been disturbed. Like an anthill that's been kicked, the commentariat complex is scattering its ants, frenzied and confused, crawling all over the pages of British newspapers and the airwaves, warning that a merciless McCarthyite campaign is under way against men. All men.

If you think this is hyperbole, you would be forgiven. I quote, in the *Telegraph*, Charles Moore declares that the women are "now on top," and hopes that they will share power equally with men, not "crush" them. In the *Mail*, we are spoilt for choice, but let's go with Peter Hitchens' (amazing even for him) logic that all that women gain from all this "squawking" about sex pests is a niqab.

In the avant garde of this movement was—of course, predictably—Giles Coren, who expressed resigned confusion about how one is to navigate this scary new world without accidentally sexually assaulting someone. Rod Liddle, in the least surprising take ever, wonders if women are hardwired to be attracted to powerful men. Brendan O'Neill called it a "sexual inquisition," saying it was a "sinister menace to democracy."

To the usual suspects, we can add Michael White—once of this parish—on Radio 4 calling Westminster female reporters "predators," David Goodhart tweeting that the debate is a "metropolitan one" that fails to distinguish hand on knee/sleazebag behaviour from rape/serious intimidation, and various others on panel shows and interviews.

While some of these men are cynical professional trolls posing as contrarians because they'd rather be wrong than irrelevant, the response en masse is actually not that much of a pose. They really do think that this current furore is a disaster, and that things are completely out of control.

There is now a well-worn perch for such men who pop up to push back against progressive agendas. But we are now dealing with a countermovement that is doing the work of the resistance as if it were a coordinated propaganda campaign. A helpful way to look at this phenomenon is to see these people less as thinking individuals with agency, but as organisms on top of a food chain reacting with instinctive self-preservation to what they perceive to be an existential threat.

Something deep in their DNA is telling them that their status is unearned: it is just a fact of biology and social conditioning. It is why they have their jobs and their social status, despite not doing very much to uniquely distinguish them from others apart from their gender and class access. The weakness they project is very real.

And, yes, the women too. Jan Moir, Melanie Philips, Anne Leslie, they also—like women who vote for self-declared misogynists everywhere—are willing to trade in their group rights in order to secure their individual privileges. The patriarchy is a sophisticated system that survives because it creates enough winners who have a vested interest in maintaining it. As is the case with any entrenched political order, when it is challenged it is always those with the most to lose, those who don't have the skills to function outside, who kick back the hardest.

And so, yes, it must all be a gross overreaction. Acts of sexual harassment must all be collapsed to the most anodyne in order to minimise what is a very serious problem that goes well beyond the touch of an elbow. The language of the witch-hunt is a giveaway. It betrays an understanding that if any of these allegations are taken seriously, then so much entitled behaviour needs to be unlearned. The Humbling must not come to pass.

That is why Michael Fallon's resignation was reduced to merely a hand on the knee, which has now somehow become the motif for the entire slew of assault allegations. You would think that what precipitated this entire moment is a rash of knee touching (as if that also is fine and "just courting"), as opposed to allegations of rape in some cases, and unwelcome sexual advances that include lunging at women from the Westminster lobby.

Brave women all over the world are coming out to share painful, confusing, even damaging experiences; and many men of influence are responding by trying to render their collective efforts stillborn. All these columns, all these interviews and frenzied tweets ask: "But how are we to survive if there are rules?"

The answer is, they don't. And they know it. By striving to maintain the status quo they are willing to sabotage what could be a profound shift in a toxic culture, and instead prop up a system that ensures women remain vulnerable to assault. A hand on a knee does not a sexual harassment epidemic make, but a group of influential men choosing to think that is all that is happening certainly maintains fertile ground where would-be harassers can continue to thrive.

EVALUATING THE AUTHOR'S ARGUMENTS:

In this viewpoint, Nesrine Malik argues that people criticizing the #MeToo movement are trying to maintain their own power. How does she support this viewpoint? Does it seem likely that she has correctly identified the issue?

Viewpoint
5

Hero or Villain? It Depends on Who You Ask

Lior Zaltzman

"Women's experiences of pain, emotional and physical, are often doubted or downgraded."

In the following viewpoint, Lior Zaltzman discusses sexual harassment claims against Elie Wiesel, the famed writer, political activist, and Nobel Peace Prize recipient. The author says she typically believes accusers in these circumstances, because sexual harassment and assault are so common. Yet women are often not believed and their experiences are taken less seriously. The author says that powerful men are often flawed, and we should be able to acknowledge their bad qualities along with their good ones. Lior Zaltzman is a writer for the Jewish Telegraphic Agency, a news source that focuses on "issues of Jewish interest and concern."

AS YOU READ, CONSIDER THE FOLLOWING QUESTIONS:
1. Why is this author not generally surprised when people are accused of sexual harassment?
2. Is it more likely that a man will be falsely accused of sexual assault, or that a man will not be convicted for a sexual assault he committed, according to the author?
3. How does power play into sexual assault, according to the viewpoint?

"I Believe the Woman Who Accused Elie Wiesel of Sexual Assault," by Lior Zaltzman, This article originally published in JTA (Jewish Telegraphic Agency), October 26, 2017. https://www.jta.org/2017/10/25/news-opinion/united-states/heres-why-i-believed-elie-wiesels-accuser.

The public does not want to believe that people they consider heroes, whether it's Elie Wiesel, their favorite actor, or their local minister, are capable of abhorrent behavior.

W hen I read the headline of Jenny Listman's *Medium* piece—"When I Was Nineteen Years Old, Elie Wiesel Grabbed My A—" —I decided not to click on it.

It wasn't because of any judgment I passed on her or the veracity of her claim. But the bluntness and clarity of her headline was, in the worst of ways, transporting—or as the youth like to say, triggering.

Not having even read it, I knew I believed it, believed her. I believed that as a 19-year-old attending a Jewish fundraiser in 1989, she was fondled by the Nobel laureate and Holocaust survivor as they posed for a group photograph.

Now I'd like to clarify that I don't think that just because I believe something, there is an obligation for news outlets like JTA to publish a story about it. We need to be thoughtful before we publish anything, especially something so serious as an allegation of unwanted sexual contact. We need to confirm certain basic facts: that the accusers are who they say they are, that they were where they claimed to be—and, when possible, get a response from the other side.

But as a woman, whenever I can, I make the choice to believe victims. I know how important it is to stand in solidarity with other women when so often our experiences are less likely to be believed. What has been especially surprising about the rise of #MeToo, the popular internet campaign that has victims of sexual assault and harassment sharing their experiences, has been the incredulous response from men. We have been telling our experiences for months and years, yet men still insist they did not know.

From my own experiences and what I've heard from other women, queer and non-binary people, I know just how common sexual harassment and assault are. They are carried out by strangers in the street and by men we believed in, who we thought were "good guys." Which is why these allegations are never surprising, to me at least.

Another thing that was not surprising to me was the propensity —especially by men (and of course by some women)—to doubt Listman's story and put her down for telling it.

Even in Listman's own tale, the response from her then-boyfriend is particularly telling: When she tells him about Wiesel squeezing her behind, he responds with incredulity. "He must have had his hand on your waist," he says. "Are you sure?"

Women's experiences of pain, emotional and physical, are often doubted or downgraded. Recent studies show that women are 13 to 24 percent less likely to be treated with opioids for pain than men, and that they have to wait longer to receive pain medication in emergency rooms. Our pain, quite literally, is taken less seriously.

I've seen people dissecting Listman's pain and trauma, so clearly depicted in her *Medium* piece, in the most ungenerous of ways. They'll say that she couldn't have been so traumatized by an action as minor as having her butt squeezed. It seems to me just another case of us doubting women's pain.

I worry that in reporting the onslaught of stories on sexual assault, harassment and rape, we all become accountants of pain or gravity. Stories like those of Harvey Weinstein and James Toback, of Bill O'Reilly and Terry Richardson, offer gruesome accounts of serial harassment, abuse and assault. There is wide consensus that these serial predators should get what they deserve. But if someone carries out an act of sexual assault only once, is it any less of a violation? In only reporting the "major" offenders, are we saying the isolated incidents are somehow OK?

According to a federally funded study, the prevalence of false reporting in cases of sexual assault is between 2 and 10 percent. Despite those incredibly low numbers, according to the study, survivors who come forward often "face scrutiny or encounter barriers" from investigators. You know what has a high likelihood? Women not reporting assault and men never being convicted for sexual assault.

As to the conversation about Elie Wiesel's "legacy"—the legacies of great men and women are always more complicated than we are comfortable admitting. And the legacies of men with power are often intertwined with abuses of that power.

There is nothing "Jewish" about the scandals surrounding Weinstein or Toback, or the allegation about Elie Wiesel—except to the degree that the Jewish media claim them as members of the "community." Theirs are stories about men in positions of power abusing the less powerful or the powerless. That's what binds the narratives pouring forth from women on Facebook and the mainstream media. We should be able to acknowledge the legacy of a man like Wiesel without ignoring the possibility that he was flawed.

But the comments about protecting the legacy of Elie Wiesel are, intentionally or not, upholding another legacy: the legacy of believing men over women and sweeping the truths of women under the carpet.

EVALUATING THE AUTHOR'S ARGUMENTS:

In this viewpoint, Lior Zaltzman says that women's pain is often discounted and women are often not believed. How is this likely to affect people's responses to women accusing men of sexual harassment or assault? Have you noticed a difference in the way people respond to claims by women versus men?

Facts About Accusations Against Public Figures

Editor's note: These facts can be used in reports to add credibility when making important points or claims.

Terms to Know

The dictionary defines **harassment** as aggressive pressure or intimidation. When someone creates an unpleasant or hostile situation for another, that is harassment. Threats, name-calling, and ridicule are examples of harassment. However, the law has a more specific criteria. Laws vary by state, but some features are common. Typically it is not enough for the behavior to make the workplace unpleasant. It must be so unpleasant that a reasonable person would consider it intimidating, hostile, or abusive. A single incident usually would not be considered harassment unless it is extremely serious. In the case of harassment, the harasser is personally liable and may be sued.

The US Equal Employment Opportunity Commission explains **sexual harassment** as follows:

- It is unlawful to harass a person (an applicant or employee) because of that person's sex. Harassment can include "sexual harassment" or unwelcome sexual advances, requests for sexual favors, and other verbal or physical harassment of a sexual nature.
- Harassment does not have to be of a sexual nature, however, and can include offensive remarks about a person's sex. For example, it is illegal to harass a woman by making offensive comments about women in general.
- Both victim and the harasser can be either a woman or a man, and the victim and harasser can be the same sex.
- Although the law doesn't prohibit simple teasing, offhand comments, or isolated incidents that are not very serious, harassment is illegal when it is so frequent or severe that it creates a hostile or offensive work environment or when it results in an

adverse employment decision (such as the victim being fired or demoted).

- The harasser can be the victim's supervisor, a supervisor in another area, a co-worker, or someone who is not an employee of the employer, such as a client or customer.

Discrimination is defined as the unfair treatment of different people or things. Discrimination often happens on the grounds of factors such as race, sex, or age. It is illegal for an employer to treat an employee unfairly because they are a member of certain groups. For example, if someone is fired because she is a woman, that is discrimination. The employer may be held liable for the actions of an employee who discriminates.

Workplace harassment and discrimination can affect people based on race, ethnicity, sexual orientation and gender identity. Not all of these forms of harassment have not been widely studied. However, some polls suggest that they are at least as common as sexual harassment. People who fit more than one category, such as women of color, may face higher rates of harassment. Workplace harassment can range from rude jokes to death threats and assaults.

Bullying is not illegal unless it crosses over into other illegal behavior. For example, if someone is bullied because of their race or sex, that may be harassment under the law.

The law also defines **sexual assault**. Sexual assault may take several forms:

- Contact with genitalia, breast, buttocks, or other intimate body parts
- Exposure of genitalia, breast, buttocks, or other intimate body parts
- Penetration of a body part by another body part or by an object

The legal punishment for sexual assault may vary. It depends on the state's laws and the circumstances of the crime. Maximum punishments may be from 6 months to 25 years in jail. The judge has some flexibility in determining the sentence. Someone convicted of sexual assault may be put on probation or allowed to go free.

The **#MeToo** movement brought awareness to the pervasive problem of sexual harassment. The hash tag started with Tarana Burke, an

African American civil rights activist, in 2006. In 2017, American actress and activist Alyssa Milano used it in a Twitter campaign. The movement gained widespread attention in the following weeks. Thousands of women shared their stories. They described how sexual harassment harmed their careers or affected them emotionally. The attention encouraged people to see how serious sexual harassment and sexual violence are. This led to more recognition and social change. Some powerful men lost their jobs after accusations of sexual harassment.

Women in the Workforce

The US has 74.6 million women in the civilian (nonmilitary) labor force. Women make up 47 percent of the total US workforce, according to the US Department of Labor. The largest percentage of women, 40.6 percent, work in management, professional, and related occupations.

The range of occupations women workers hold has expanded. Women have especially gained in professional and managerial occupations. Still, women and men are disproportionately found in some fields. In management, women make up 74 percent of human resources managers but only 27 percent of chief executives. Women are underrepresented in STEM occupations. Their numbers have actually declined in the computer field since 1990. Sexual harassment can happen in any field but may be more common when most coworkers are male.

Sexual Harassment and Assault

Several polls have asked whether people have been sexually harassed or assaulted. Results vary depending on how questions are worded and other factors. In one survey, 81 percent of women said they had experienced some form of sexual harassment or assault in their lives. Among men, 43 percent said the same. Many victims experienced depression or anxiety as a result.

Some polls focus specifically on workplace harassment. These may ask if women have been sexually harassed or abused at work or by someone from their workplace. In various polls, between 22 and 35 percent of woman have said yes. Numbers may vary depending on how sexual harassment is defined.

Stop Street Harassment released a nationwide survey of harassment and assault in 2018. Verbal harassment was most common. It was reported by 77 percent of women and 34 percent of men. Physical harassment was reported by 62 percent of women and 26 percent of men. Physical included unwelcome sexual touching, being followed, and being shown someone's genitals against their will. People also experience harassment by text, phone, or online. This was reported by 41 percent of women and 22 percent of men. Finally, 27 percent of women and 7 percent of men said they had been sexually assaulted.

Women and men vary to some extent in what they consider harassment. In one poll, 96 percent of women and 86 percent of men said "touching or groping" counted as harassment. For "making sexual comments about looks or body," 86 percent of women and 70 percent of men thought that was harassment. Most women and men did not think that asking a woman on a date was harassment. However, what if the person persisted in asking someone out after being told no? Then 58 percent of women and 47 percent of men did think it was harassment.

Different age groups have different opinions on how much of a problem sexual harassment is. One survey asked if "sexual harassment happens in almost all or most workplaces." Among women 18 to 49 years old, 78 percent said yes. Among women 50 or older, only 64 percent said yes. A similar difference was found in men's responses. Among men 18 to 49 years old, 68 percent said yes. Among men 50 or older, only 55 percent said yes. Several factors may contribute to the differences based on age. Younger people may be more often victims of harassment. They may talk more openly about harassment they experience or witness. They may also have different opinions about what behavior is considered harassment.

An estimated 63 percent of sexual assaults are never reported to the police. Victims may suffer emotions that make it hard for them to talk about the experience. They may be afraid of the physical exam designed to find evidence of assault. They may want to avoid answering personal questions. They may also be afraid of repercussions from family, friends, or coworkers. This is especially common if the assault involved someone from that group.

It is difficult to determine the exact number of false accusations of sexual assault. Some estimates range from 2 percent to 10 percent. However, those numbers may be higher than reality. Statistics can include cases where victims decided not to cooperate, or cases without enough evidence to proceed to prosecution. As a result, many reports may be classified as false when they were in fact true but unproven. This is according to a report published by the National Sexual Violence Resource Center.

Organizations to Contact

The editors have compiled the following list of organizations concerned with the issues debated in this book. The descriptions are derived from materials provided by the organizations. All have publications or information available for interested readers. The list was compiled on the date of publication of the present volume; the information provided here may change. Be aware that many organizations take several weeks or longer to respond to inquiries, so allow as much time as possible for the receipt of requested materials.

The American Association of University Women (AAUW)
1310 L St. NW, Suite 1000, Washington, DC 20005
(800) 326-2289
email: connect@aauw.org
website: www.aauw.org
An organization that promotes equity and education for women and girls. AAUW members address educational, social, economic, and political issues. The website provides information on knowing your rights on campus and at work.

Defend Yourself
(301) 608-3708
email: lauren@defendyourself.org
website: www.defendyourself.org
Defend Yourself works to empower people, especially women and LGBTQ people, to end violence. Classes teach techniques for dealing with everything from bothersome people to physical attacks. The website includes Resources and an advice section to "Learn something now."

Girls Fight Back
(866) 769-9037
website: www.girlsfightback.com/
Girls Fight Back provides training for young women to learn violence

prevention and self-defense. Students Fight Back offers the same basic skills, for any gender. The website offers information on how to set up a demonstration, as well as links to resources.

Girls for Gender Equity (GGE)
25 Chapel St., Suite 1006, Brooklyn, NY 11201
(718) 857-1393
website: www.ggenyc.org/
Girls for Gender Equity works to end gender-based violence, especially for girls and women of color. Priorities are education, organizing, and physical fitness. On the website, find articles, a blog, and ways to get involved.

International Center for Research on Women (ICRW)
1120 20th St. NW, Suite 500 N, Washington, D.C. 20036
(202) 797-0007
email: info@icrw.org
website: www.icrw.org
ICRW's mission is to advance gender equality. The organization uses research to find the best answers to the issues facing women and girls. ICRW then works with advocates and leaders to develop solutions. The website provides resources and publications.

MasculinityU
(202) 656-4805
email: booking@masculinityu.com
website: www.masculinityu.com
MasculinityU is a coalition working to bring change to US communities, colleges, states, and the country. It offers a national speakers bureau, curriculum development, advocacy and programmatic consulting, and guided facilitation.

Men Stopping Violence
2785 Lawrenceville Hwy., Suite 112, Decatur, GA 30033
(866) 717-9317
website: www.menstoppingviolence.org/
Men Stopping Violence organizes men to end male violence against

women and girls. The group uses training programs and advocacy. It states, "Social justice work in the areas of race, class, gender, age, and sexual orientation are all critical to ending violence against women."

The National Organization for Women (NOW)
1100 H St. NW, Suite 300, Washington, DC 20005
(202) 628-8669
website: www.now.org/
NOW is an advocacy organization. Its goals include defending reproductive rights, fighting economic inequality, and ending discrimination and violence against women and girls. It's website offers information on the group's campaigns, background on the issues, and ways to get involved.

RAINN (Rape, Abuse & Incest National Network)
1220 L St. NW, Washington, DC 20005
(202) 544-1034
website: www.rainn.org
RAINN carries out programs to prevent sexual violence and support survivors. The website provides information on sexual assaults, including safety planning, steps to take after an assault, and reporting to law enforcement. The site also has links to telephone hotlines and other means of getting support after an assault.

Women's Media Center (WMC)
PO Box 70967, Washington, DC 20024-0967
(202) 855-3300
email: wmcdc@womensmediacenter.com
website: www.womensmediacenter.com
WMC works toward media equality using research, original stories and articles, promotion of women experts, and media training. It includes WMC Fbomb, an intersectional teen feminist media platform created by and for socially conscious youth.

For Further Reading

Books

Ballman, Donna. *Stand Up For Yourself Without Getting Fired: Resolve Workplace Crises Before You Quit, Get Axed or Sue the Bastards.* Wayne, NJ: Career Press, 2012.

Prepare for your working future by understanding how to face tough situations. The author addresses hostile workplaces as well as other career situations.

Carlson, Gretchen. *Be Fierce: Stop Harassment and Take Your Power Back.* Nashville, TN: Center Street, 2017.

A journalist shares her own experiences and that of other women. She includes guidelines for women to empower themselves in the workplace or on a college campus.

Erps, George. *Sexual Harassment: One Man's Journey.* Independently published, 2017.

What happens when an innocent man is attacked for sexual harassment? This book follows a man who tries to navigate the legal system and clear his name.

Henter, Charles. *Know Your Rights: Easy Employment Law for Employees.* Independently published, 2013.

The author uses a conversational tone to explain employment law so everyone can know their basic rights.

Paludi, Michele A. and Jennifer L. Martin. *Sexual Harassment in Education and Work Settings: Current Research and Best Practices for Prevention (Women's Psychology).* Santa Barbara, CA: 2015.

This title addresses current legal and psychological issues involved in campus and workplace violence. It offers practices for organizations seeking to prevent and respond to sexual misconduct.

Still-Rolin, Julie. *The End Game: A Guide for Those Who Truly Want to End Sexual Harassment*. Independently published, 2017.

> An examination of sexual harassment and how to prevent and address it. The book includes role-playing training techniques to help people handle sexual harassment.

Strauss, Susan. *Sexual Harassment and Bullying: A Guide to Keeping Kids Safe and Holding Schools Accountable*. Lanham, MD: Rowman & Littlefield Publishers, 2013.

> This book contrasts bullying and sexual harassment as they relate to the law and their impact on children. The author shares case studies and provides resources for readers.

Whittenbury, Beth K. *The Student's Guide to Preventing Sexual Harassment in the Workplace*. Independently published, 2013.

> This title is designed for students studying business law or employment law. It addresses how organizations and individuals can prevent sexual harassment in the workplace.

Periodicals and Internet Sources

Anonymous. "Believe Her*," The Order of the White Feather, https://wearawhitefeather.wordpress.com/

Brook, Tom Vanden. "Sexual Harassment, Racism and a Secret Settlement at the 'Crossroads of the Marine Corps,' Report Shows," *USA TODAY*, March 7, 2018.

Brown, Jonathan. "The Presumption of Innocence When Too Many Victims Go Unheard." Al-Madina Institute, Nov. 14, 2017. http://almadinainstitute.org/blog/the-presumption-of-innocence-when-too-many-victims-go-unheard/

Doyle, Sady. "Despite What You May Have Heard, 'Believe Women' Has Never Meant 'Ignore Facts,'" *Elle*, Nov. 29, 2017. https://www.elle.com/culture/career-politics/a13977980/me-too-movement-false-accusations-believe-women/

Harnish, Amelia. "The Post-Weinstein Reckoning: What Do We Do Now?" Refinery29, Nov. 29, 2017. https://www.refinery29 .com/2017/11/182877/after-me-too-punishment-accountability-what-to-do-next

Jackson, Ben. "Witch Hunts for "Racists" and "Sexists" in the US Is Getting Out of Control," *PanAm Post*, Aug. 21, 2017. https:// panampost.com/ben-jackson/2017/08/21/how-the-epidemic-of-witch-hunting-for-bigots-is-ruining-lives-without-warrant/

Lostetter, Marina J. "Moral, Ethical, Legal: What's the Difference?" A Little Lost, Mar. 14, 2012. https://lostetter.wordpress .com/2012/03/14/moral-ethical-legal-whats-the-difference/

Malone, Noreen. "'I'm No Longer Afraid': 35 Women Tell Their Stories about Being Assaulted by Bill Cosby, and the Culture That Wouldn't Listen," *New York*, July 26, 2015. https://www.thecut.com/2015/07/ bill-cosbys-accusers-speak-out.html

McAllister, D.C. "It's Not Up To Women To End Sexual Harassment," Apr. 26, 2017. *The Federalist*. http://thefederalist.com/2017/04/26/ not-women-end-sexual-harassment/

Messina, Toni. "The Sexual Harassment Dilemma," Above the Law, Nov. 13, 2017. https://abovethelaw.com/2017/11/the-sexual-harassment-dilemma/

North, Anna. "Want to Stop Sexual Harassment? Start Helping Women." *Vox*, Nov. 9, 2017. https://www.vox.com/identi-ties/2017/11/9/16600170/sexual-harassment-harvey-weinstein-workplace

Nwanevu, Osita. "Bret Stephens' Mob Mentality," *Slate*, Feb. 12, 2018. https://slate.com/news-and-politics/2018/02/bret-stephens-mob-mentality.html

Oluo, Ijeoma. "Due Process Is Needed for Sexual Harassment Accusations, but for Whom," *The Establishment*, Nov. 20, 2017. https:// theestablishment.co/due-process-is-needed-for-sexual-harassment-accusations-but-for-whom-968e7c81e6d6

Pember, Mary Annette. "Sherman Alexie and the Longest Running #MeToo Movement in History," *Rewire*, Mar 2, 2018. https://rewire.news/article/2018/03/02/sherman-alexie-longest-running-me-too-movement-history/

Rhoades, Gary. "Sexual Harassment and Group Punishment," *Inside Higher Ed*, Feb. 12, 2009. https://www.insidehighered.com/views/2009/02/12/sexual-harassment-and-group-punishment

Sikka, Madhulika. "(Not) a Vindication of the Rights of Women," *The Daily Beast*, Dec. 3, 2017. https://www.thedailybeast.com/not-a-vindication-of-the-rights-of-women

Steinberg, Brian. "Sexual Harassment Scandals Force Media Companies to Become the News," *Variety*, Dec. 13, 2017. http://variety.com/2017/tv/news/sexual-harassment-scandals-media-companies-news-1202638306/

Traister, Rebecca. "Our National Narratives Are Still Being Shaped by Lecherous, Powerful Men," *New York Magazine*. Oct. 27, 2017. https://www.thecut.com/2017/10/halperin-wieseltier-weinstein-powerful-lecherous-men.html

Young, Cathy. "Crying Rape," *Slate*, Sep. 18, 2014. http://www.slate.com/articles/double_x/doublex/2014/09/false_rape_accusations_why_must_be_pretend_they_never_happen.html

Websites

A CALL TO MEN (www.acalltomen.org)

A CALL TO MEN works with corporations, organizations and the government to provide education and training to prevent sexual harassment in the workplace. The website offers information on youth development programs. The online blog offers thoughts on manhood, toxic masculinity, ways to prevent sexual harassment, and more.

Geek Feminism Wiki (geekfeminism.wikia.com)

A resource for and about women in geek communities. The site has basic information about feminism, while articles and blog posts address a variety of topics relating to feminism and sexism. Resources include advice on effective anti-harassment policies.

Harvard Business Review (hbr.org/topic/gender)

Harvard Business Review covers many areas of business, management, and human resources. The "Gender" tag shows articles and opinion pieces on sexual harassment, #MeToo, and women in the workplace.

RAINN (www.rainn.org/)

The Rape, Abuse & Incest National Network is the largest anti-sexual assault organization in the United States. The website offers information, resources, and a help hotline.

US Equal Employment Opportunity Commission (www.eeoc.gov)

This government agency is responsible for enforcing federal laws that make it illegal to discriminate against a job applicant. Search for "sexual harassment" to bring up fact sheets, policies, and information on laws.

Index

Emin, Tracey, 66
Everyday Sexism, 42
expulsion and disenrollment, 23, 83

F
Facebook, 7, 28, 32, 85, 88, 100
Fallon, Michael, 94
false accusations, 18, 21-22, 29, 78, 80, 105
Featherstone, Vicky, 37, 39
felony crimes, 22
First Nation and Native American women writers, 47–48
Fox, Julia, 70
Fox News, 74
Franken, Al, 53-54

G
Gansworth, Eric, 48
Gauguin, Eugene Henri Paul, 65
Gay, Roxane, 71
gender discrimination, 14, 16, 56, 57, 58, 59–60, 102
Gilbey, Ryan, 63, 65
Gillibrand, Kirsten, 87
Goodhart, David, 93
Graves, Langdon, 70

H
Hill, Anita, 17, 41
Hitchcock, Alfred, 65–66
Hitchens, Peter, 93
Hughes, Scottie Nell, 76–77
Huston, John, 64

I
If I Ever Get Out of Here (Gansworth), 48
institutional racism, 47

J
Jolie, Angelina, 15, 40
Judd, Ashley, 14

K
Kassin, Saul, 24
Keillor, Garrison, 53
Kemplin, Stephanie, 53–54
kidnapping. See abduction and kidnapping
Kimmel, Michael, 41–42
Kleiner Perkins, 16
Kubrick, Stanley, 65

L
LaSalle, Devin, 22
Lauer, Matt, 58
Leclere, Margaret, 62
Levitski, Robin, 19–24
Leslie, Anne, 93–94
Liddle, Rod, 93
Listman, Jenny, 97, 98–99

M
Maher, Kevin, 65
Malik, Nesrine, 91
#MeToo, 7–8, 10, 26, 27, 28, 33, 48, 56, 57, 58–59, 60, 63, 66, 68, 70–71, 91, 92, 98, 102
Milano, Alyssa, 7, 70, 103
Moir, Jan, 93–94
Moore, Charles, 92

Picture Credits